Nº 334

Nº 403

simplehome

simplehome

calm spaces for comfortable living

mark & sally bailey

photography by Debi Treloar

LONDON · NEW YORK

Senior designer Paul Tilby
Editor Delphine Lawrance
Location research Sally Bailey, Jess Walton
Production manager Toby Marshall
Art director Leslie Harrington
Publishing director Alison Starling

Styling Mark Bailey

First published in 2009
by Ryland Peters & Small
20–21 Jockey's Fields
London WC1R 4BW
519 Broadway, 5th Floor
New York, NY 10012
www.rylandpeters.com

Text copyright © Mark and Sally Bailey 2009
Design and photographs copyright
© Ryland Peters & Small 2009

10 9 8 7 6 5

Bailey, Mark.
  Simple home : calm spaces for comfortable living
/ Mark & Sally Bailey ; photography by Debi Treloar.
      p. cm.
  Includes index.
  ISBN 978-1-84597-915-7
  1. Interior decoration--Psychological aspects. I.
Bailey, Sally. II. Treloar, Debi. III. Title. IV. Title: Calm
spaces for comfortable living.
  NK2113.B34 2009
  747--dc22

2009010301

Printed and bound in China.

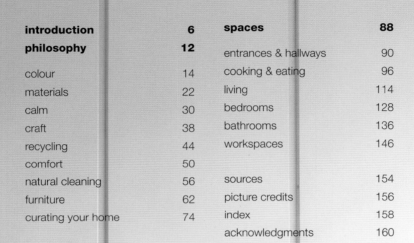

contents

introduction

The simple home is about keeping things plain and useful – it is a chance to get back to basics, to consider ideals of good design and the forgotten traditions of craftsmanship and then think how they can be adapted to a more modern approach. This way of living feels refreshing in a time when things seem to have a tendency to get over-complicated.

That is not to say the simple home has to be hard-edged

right A marble sheet propped up on two ornate but very weathered former French café table stands makes a great resting place for some daffodils and woven wicker trays.

opposite A room infused with natural daylight and clean white paint is the perfect spot for two simply upholstered white chairs to sit quietly side by side.

or overly austere, with no cats, crumbs or kids allowed. Instead, it is the key to comfortable, relaxed living – it allows for flexibility and endless options, giving you the chance to curate your home like a personal museum. Reconsider your belongings and only surround yourself with things that you really love. Objects that have been well crafted can make everyday life a pleasure; from sweeping the stairs with a beautifully constructed wooden

brush to relaxing on a soft, linen-covered sofa at the end of a hard day. The traditions that lie behind the manufacture of these things are all about using the best materials for the job, perhaps making them by hand – even if it takes longer this way, and ensuring that the end product will last for years. Well-made, well-designed things grow old gracefully. But as well as these industrious objects, be sure to include others that are cherished because they remind you of a person, place or time; these are the treasures that will make your home unique.

Another aspect of the simple home way of thinking is the ability to find beauty in the imperfections that come with age and wear and tear. Old furniture that has been loved and looked after enough to stand the test of time has a reassuring, timeless elegance, no matter how battered, scraped and scratched it may appear now. So choose pieces that have a history; not necessarily antiques but items that have been rescued and given a new purpose in life, or new furniture that has been crafted out of found objects and old pieces of wood. Such things have a natural honesty and integrity that makes them desirable rather than fashionable.

this page The essence of
simplicity in a quiet corner – two
bentwood ash stools and a
handmade porcelain lamp slung
casually over a nail. The wire
basket is filled with old lavender
twigs for a sweet-scented fire.

opposite left An unusual
twist on tradition, here old
wooden curtain rings are used
for keeping vintage linen
napkins in place.

opposite right Utensils
stored tidily in a glazed jar.
Casually posed postcards
soften the Sicilian marble.

opposite Scaffolding poles form the simple skeleton of this bed, while the nonchalantly slung, graphic handwoven textiles and white patchwork blanket make a great contrast. Ticking rugs on the floor mirror the graphic theme neatly.

below Copper piping makes a functional and honest-looking towel warmer. Strings of pebble and stone collected on beachside holidays add to its rugged charm.

Light plays an important part in a home with a pared-down, simple style – it makes your space feel clear, uncluttered, light and airy. In an understated way, a room filled with natural light will be the first thing you notice and will certainly leave a lasting impression, long after the furniture and the fixtures and fittings have faded away. Light can make an even better impression if the backdrop is calm and quiet. Choose colours that are inspired by nature rather than fashionable colour charts, or colours that just turn up from underneath layers of paint. With this in mind, the shades found in the simple home are soft and chalkily pale, but they retain a feeling of freshness that comes about when things are stored away and the space is neat, tidy and as free from clutter as possible. So once you have taken all those articles that you don't really need to the grateful ladies at the charity shop, you will need to invest in decent storage – though not just mass-produced, ugly plastic boxes. Think in a more creative way and your home will look all the better for it.

In the end, you can't really go wrong if you follow the assertion of American architect, interior designer, writer and all-round man of wisdom, Frank Lloyd Wright:

'Study nature, love nature, stay close to nature and it will never fail you.'

philosophy

colour

above A worn, weather-beaten wall, showing off its different layers of texture and subtle tones, and an old outdoor verdigris copper tap demonstrate how colours change and mature over time.

above right Piles of ticking cushions and blankets provide contrastingly sharp stripes of colour in simpler surrounds.

opposite An assortment of collected maps, photos, lumpy-textured wall and nature are all subtle ways to bring a glimpse of colour into your home.

On first glance, the simple home may appear to be devoid of colour, but that is to dismiss the subtleties of an understated, more natural approach to the subject. The colour scheme is not dictated to by the whims of what's in fashion, colour charts or the rules and regulations of the colour wheel. In this way, it is much more personal, with colour coming from the addition of one or two of your favourite things. The simple home is predominantly filled with soft colours that quietly complement each other and envelop your surroundings with a sense of calm. Think of the colours and texture of handmade paper and you'll be well on the way to the perfect palette for your home.

A subtle colour range of classic neutral colours like soft, milky whites, tree-bark beige, creamy ivory and silvery greys forms the perfect painterly backdrop to your space, bathing your home in gentle tones that generously allow other splashes of colour to take centre stage. This might be your favourite painting, a vividly printed cushion or simply a farmhouse jug of flowers.

The deliberately limited colour scheme of your walls reflects the natural, honest materials of your home – beautiful grainy wooden floors and furniture, as well as the undulations and dimples of old, worn stone and tiles. Neutral colours welcome the infusion of warmth from the tones and textures found in such enduring signs of construction.

Choosing white to paint your walls is not a step backwards into the glaringly harsh white of monochrome, minimalist colour schemes. The look is easily softened by what you choose to surround yourself with; go for slubby linens or chunkily hand-knitted blankets coloured with natural dyes rather than the hard edges of minimalist furniture (or lack of it). Sunlight plays a large part too, bringing out the best in the world of white. With light falling through your windows, the varieties of tone become almost infinite; think of white cotton sheets drying in the sunlight and flapping in the breeze. White and sunlight are the best of flexible friends, with white changing tone depending on the time of day, like the colours of nature changing depending on the season.

Other colours that work well with soft neutrals are generally those that are mixed with generous quantities of white. Think back to days at school spent mixing paints in a palette – you hardly need to add any coloured pigment to give white a delicious hint of something else. These colours have a faded feeling of worn-out softness; just like a child's soft toy that has been washed hundreds of times but remains the favourite among the hoards of shinier plastic toys, or comforting milky drinks that warm your hands in the depths of winter.

opposite left The beautifully textured wall is almost like an Impressionist painting of a cloudy sky. The soft folds of the loosely covered armchair enhance the subtle blue shades.

opposite centre Artworks are another way to introduce small flashes of colour into the home.

opposite right The stripey grain of this white-washed table shows off the surprisingly myriad tones of white, while a platter of old varieties of English apples adds another gently colourful element.

this page A gently faded denim-covered armchair looks like the perfect spot to rest by the creamy Aga. Its washed-out blues are the perfect partner to the terracotta floor tiles.

You are unlikely to find huge expanses of shout-out-loud bright colours in the simple home. There might be the odd burst of it here and there, sometimes planned or sometimes more unexpectedly found by chance – maybe discovered hidden under layers of flaky paint – or more deliberately in the detail of a cushion or cosy woollen throw. Nature is also a good place to start when considering flashes of brighter bits of colour. Think about how colour changes as things age – like the way copper oxidizes when left to the elements, going from bright shiny orange to soft verdigris (like the Statue of Liberty). Or bring in the innate brightness of nature such as the crazily dazzling orange of

CHOOSE COLOURS THAT ARE INSPIRED BY NATURE RATHER THAN FASHIONABLE COLOUR CHARTS.

autumn leaves, acidic lemony yellows of old-fashioned varieties of apples or bright bunches of flowers casually displayed in old French confit jars. These small splashes of colour add contrast to the larger areas of chalky whites, soft greys and comforting light browns, but at the same time they make you even more aware of the gentleness of your overall colour scheme. The neutral colours harmonize with the brighter flashes of colour and give you and your home a feeling of relaxation and well-being.

above A set of monochrome plates sits on an unusual patchwork tablecloth. The ensemble is softened by the dried grasses.

left A worn music case and shiny boots create a simple still life.

opposite The vivid shades of autumn bring bold colours into the home – the fig leaves are in fact made of rusting steel.

above left Concertina paper lanterns, left undecorated, are hung on long, supple bamboo canes to create an unusual point of interest on a gently sloping ceiling.

above centre The dappled patchwork of colours of these steel bistro chairs shows the licks of paint lavished on them over time and are beautiful signs of age, which should not be shied away from.

above right The sturdy bench against a weathered wall reveals the amazing textures of stone.

opposite With its turned brass handle, this door shows the honesty of wood as it wears through use.

We don't often consider the materials our houses are made from; we notice them every now and then as we slide our hands along a smooth wooden banister or feel a cool tiled floor under bare feet as we run to collect the pile of post pushed through the letterbox. In the simple home, however, the materials of construction are proudly displayed rather than hidden away under layers of paint and plaster. Stone floors and fireplaces, bare, uncovered brickwork, old tiles, wooden floors, doors and beams are star materials – especially when set off by softly neutral colours. In previous years they would have been hidden or disguised; now is the time to restore them to their former glory and proudly reveal the inner workings of your house.

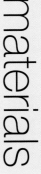
materials

WOOD AND STONE ARE HARD-WEARING, ROUGH, TOUGH MATERIALS. THEY ARE WELL AND TRULY CAPABLE OF STANDING THE TEST OF TIME.

Floors and walls form the bare bones of your home – celebrate their construction, leaving them unpainted or scraping off layers of paint and plaster to reveal their inner beauty. It is an honest way to 'decorate', despite being almost the exact opposite of decoration. Leaving them freshly unadorned shows what your home has been through before you came along and how these ancient materials are well and truly capable of standing the test of time and ever-demanding families.

Scratches, flaky paint, speckles, freckles, raw edges and nail and pin heads left on display are the hallmarks of authenticity and craftsmanship – these are signs of age and belong to materials that have been well cared for, repaired and not left to quietly rot. While wood and stone are hard-wearing, rough, tough materials, they do have their points of weakness and require a little TLC. Their continued existence shows that they've been loved and this gives us a cosy warm glow inside.

above left A simple wooden shelf with metal rod supports is home to a pile of Vietnamese bamboo sieves. The little bird on a wire adds humorous detail.

above right Unusually curvaceous apothecary bottles with stemmed bases hold linear-looking twigs, bringing the more delicate materials of nature into the home.

opposite Contrasting materials holding kindling work well together. The wirework basket was rescued from an abandoned park rubbish bin.

Invite more modern materials into your home too; the unexpected combinations of textures they introduce make our homes a sensory pleasure. Recycled rubber has an honest durability and is up to the hardest of tasks in your home. Stainless steel and aluminium are other materials that are ignored at your peril. They are shiny but not too shiny or brash, and provide the perfect contrast to more roughly hewn materials. Another up-and-coming star is concrete, somewhat surprisingly if you have memories of brutalist 1960s architecture. Rugged-looking poured concrete makes for a floor with an amazing surface.

When looking for furniture, choose skeletal wooden chairs and go for tables either with skinny, tapered legs or sturdy, extra-chunky ones – extremes like these make much more of a statement than in-between compromises. Another surprising material to consider is paper, such as paper lanterns or lampshades. Its delicate nature plays with the sturdiness of other, more solid materials in the home.

MATERIALS OF CONSTRUCTION ARE PROUDLY DISPLAYED RATHER THAN BEING HIDDEN AWAY UNDER LAYERS OF PAINT AND PLASTER.

above Wood shows its signs of age and wear and tear with pride – whatever you do, don't cover them up with new paint.

right A sliding door made from sturdy sheet metal panels has been brushed with tourmaline to make it less shiny and to speed up the aging process.

far right A closer view of the door shows how the panels have been riveted together. Delicate paper decorations soften the industrial backdrop.

opposite Scratchy-looking rusty metal and concrete contrast beautifully with the polished floor, glass balustrade and smooth cupboard doors.

this page The mixture of natural shapes and textures creates a restful corner in this room. The unruly swirl of twigs in the fireplace provides another piece of nature in the home.

opposite right Wonky, hand-thrown porcelain vases by Bridget Tennant crowd together on a simple angular fireplace. Light diffusing through Perspex shades adds to the sense of calm pervading the room.

opposite left A sculptural paper shade hung from a length of bamboo.

We seem to be so busy all the time, rushing around with long lists of things to do. The constant surrounding bombardment of random snippets of noise only serves to raise our stress levels further still. With this going on around us every day, our homes really need to be a haven of tranquillity and relaxation. The good news is that if you choose to create an interior that embraces the idea of simplicity, you will infuse your home with a sense of calm without really having to think too much about it.

The ice cream-soft colour scheme of the simple home, with its tones of whites, honey browns and silvery greys, goes a long way to creating this tranquil idyll. These

colours are easy on the eye and gently whisper in contrast to the bright colours that shout at us during our working day. Choosing tones that are close together in the colour spectrum creates a feeling of harmony, as nothing jars or leaps out at us. Instead, they relax the senses, and as the colours react to the differing qualities of seasonal daylight, they can feel either cosy and warming like a creamy lambswool sweater or, on a hot day, deliciously cool.

calm

far left A late-Victorian daybed re-upholstered in plain linen provides a place of rest by the window. The elaborately turned table adds to the air of refined elegance, but the bare washed floorboards ensure that the room remains fuss-free.

left The theme of relaxed elegance is continued in this room, with a squashy-looking sofa and simple metal-framed daybed piled with silky wheat-filled cushions and blankets. The tones of white add to the sense of calm.

YOUR VERY FAVOURITE THINGS, HOWEVER INSIGNIFICANT THEY MAY SEEM, SHOULD BE WELL MADE AND DO THEIR JOB WITHOUT BEING OSTENTATIOUS.

Taking time to find the beauty in small, seemingly ordinary things makes daily life a pleasure. Make sure that absolutely everything in your home has a place in your heart. Your very favourite things, however insignificant they may seem, should be well made and do their job without being ostentatious. Don't save your good taste for books and paintings; everyday items such as soft, fluffy piles of towels in the bathrooom or the mug you drink your morning coffee from can bring you joy. In this way, the simple act of opening a cupboard can make you smile, be it a cupboard stacked with sheets and blankets in your favourite colour combinations, a shelf of simple Japanese-looking drinking vessels or neat piles of monochrome plates and bowls.

this page The sheer curtain, subtly embroidered with a quote from writer and film-maker Marcel Pagnol, softens the light flooding through the large window and creates a tranquil setting for reading. The naturally curving stool has been hand-wrapped with thick, undyed twine.

opposite A paint-splattered ladder resting against a plain white wall contrasts well with the shelves holding 'Seven Cups on Floating Grounds' by ceramicist Julian Stair.

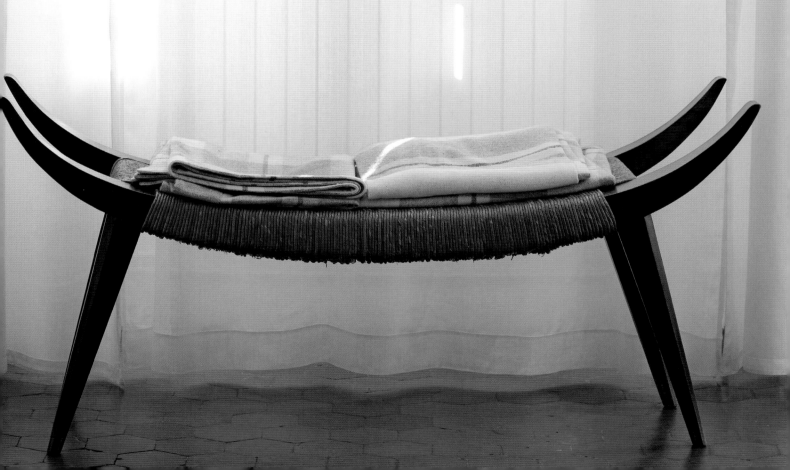

"les mots qui ont en son noble contiennent toujours de belles images."

Marcel Pagnol

DECORATING YOUR HOME WITH HANDMADE OBJECTS MAKES YOU FEEL GOOD – THEY TAKE TIME TO CREATE AND PROMOTE A SENSE OF PEACE.

above left The clean lines of the room remain unbroken by leaning the prints on the table rather than a more conventional wall display.

above right Delicate flowers contrast well with a sturdy, recycled rubber bucket.

opposite The symmetry of this space creates a wonderful feeling of serenity, enhanced all the more by the subdued colours and soft textures.

The well-worn materials of your home have an easy, timeless grace, and as well as reminding us of a time when life wasn't so hectic, they provide us with a connection to nature. Sitting on a beautiful wooden floor transports us back to the last time we took a moment to sit under a tree in a sunny park. Collections of pebbles and seashells from summers spent beachcombing have a similarly calming effect. Decorating your home with one or two handmade objects makes you feel good; they take time to create, and this quality promotes a sense of peace. Having a disciplined cleaning routine and well-considered storage helps your home to be clutter free, clean and tidy. As a result you get a cleansing, calming space that is liberated from reminders of household chores yet to be done. The same goes for overly embellished interiors that are too fussy or frilly; all that frippery gets in the way.

Purposefully create your own small oasis of calm. All it takes is a pile of soft, unbleached cotton cushions in a cosy corner, or a favourite armchair placed in a daylight-infused room, with sheer curtains wafting in the breeze. They're perfect places to sit and quietly take in your home's beauty.

opposite These handwoven twiggy platters highlight the untamed nature of craft. Set on a smooth marble surface with an elaborate base, their wonky charm is all the more evident.

right Redundant pieces of print block have found the perfect resting place in a hand-carved Ethiopian wooden vessel, which was probably used for some kind of game in its former life.

far right Mahatma Ghandi watches over piles of hand-stitched books covered in offcuts of raw Indian cotton.

below An old tailor's dummy is put to good use as a stand for strings of jewellery.

When thinking about craft and handmade objects, it's important to get as far away from memories of garish crocheted tea cosies at Sunday craft fairs as possible. These days, craft can be viewed as a rebellion against the ubiquity of mass production. We've all had more than enough of seeing the same things over and over, in one home to the next, with the same short life span. Choosing something handmade by an artisan is a celebration of individuality, durability and simple beauty.

craft

above Exquisite examples of the highest form of quality craftsmanship. A collection of plain, unglazed ceramic vessels and sculptural looking teapots by Julian Stair. The centre teapot sports a wisteria handle. The pared-down palette and simple shapes lend these beautiful pots a refined air.

right Ever so slightly wonky, tall, skinny, fat, thin and tiny porcelain vases hand thrown by Bridget Tennant. Together they create a monumental, almost Stonehenge-like display.

CHOOSING SOMETHING HANDMADE BY AN ARTISAN IS A CELEBRATION OF INDIVIDUALITY, DURABILITY AND SIMPLE BEAUTY.

The influence of craft and all things handmade in the simple home can be felt in every room. Handmade objects of all shapes and sizes have a myriad of uses, from tables made from reclaimed wooden floorboards, handwoven naturally dyed textiles and tactile hand-thrown ceramics to beautifully intricate jewellery made from a collection of seed pods. These things are made to be used or worn, not just looked at; form and function go hand in hand with aesthetic pleasure. Objects such as these are what make our homes personal and unique. We generally buy something that is handcrafted because we love it and this is a big part of the simple home – to carefully choose well-made, useful things because they please us, not just because they are cheap and easily obtainable. In this way, the everyday becomes infinitely more pleasurable.

The elements of the handmade are an essential part of the ideals of the simple home. They have an inherent individuality – quirks, flaws and a certain wonkiness reveal how they have been made and set them apart from things that have been mass produced and can be found everywhere. The materials used are recognizable, honest and relate to nature: wood, glass, clay and textiles. It is clear that much thought, care, time and attention to detail have gone into the production of handmade objects and this is a large part of their appeal, as it seems to infuse them with a sense of calm and makes them a delight to use.

this page A collection of plain, antique ceramic pots. From left to right – a white stoneware cup from China, a stoneware faceted bowl from Japan, a porcelain offering plate from Korea, a stoneware amawori bottle and stoneware bowl, both from Japan and a stoneware jar from China.

right An old tin truck is neatly parked on a table made from aging pieces of wood board. The unexpected flash of orange adds a sense of fun, along with the floating globe.

far right This scratchy zinc-plated number two probably once adorned a shop front.

below A pile of handmade books covered in patchwork scraps of Indian cotton.

opposite top left These sculptural ceremonial paper hats are amazingly crafted by hand entirely out of paper.

opposite top right A cast-iron star-shaped wall plate watches over some wooden print block.

opposite centre A misty painting atop a marble fireplace.

opposite left A pair of mosaic ceramic hands by Cleo Muzzi.

opposite right A delicate pair of handmade paper wings.

DON'T RELY ON OTHER PEOPLE FOR YOUR CRAFT ITEMS; REDISCOVER SUCH OLD HOBBIES AS MAKING CARDS, KNITTING OR EMBROIDERY.

Handcrafted objects are more often than not made using traditional skills that have been handed down through the generations; by inviting craft into your home, you are keeping these old skills alive. Also, look out for things that were handmade years before, as they tend to be so well constructed that they still have a job to do today. They may need a bit of looking after to bring them back to life, but the time this takes will be well worth it. They feel good to use, some areas smoothed away where they were held by previous owners, plus they're so much more tactile than their modern-day cousins.

Some objects relating to craft may have outlived their previous use, such as wooden print block, but they remind us of an era before the digital age when processes took a little longer and our lives were less hectic. Collections of print block look lovely, with their worn and slightly ink-stained edges, and as well as their aesthetic appeal they can be used on a much smaller scale to make handmade cards – just take time out to do it! Don't rely on other people for your craft items; rediscover such old hobbies as making cards or knitting, embroidery or, if you can find the necessary facilities, ceramics. These crafts have long since shed their old-fashioned image. There are all sorts of inspirational contemporary craftspeople (or makers as they prefer to be known) out there creating amazing items. It's a much better use of time than relying on huge televisions for entertainment.

this page A classic Ercol rocking chair shows off its skeletal clean lines and looks all the more refined as it sits beside a scuffed and scratched set of drawers rescued from a workshop. A French brioche tin has been adapted to create a recycled light shade.

far left A curved wooden cupboard, once hard at work in a shop, has been stripped of its paint to show off its grainy features. It provides a resting place for tin trucks and print block made into an artwork, with its original thin print drawer acting as a frame.

left A detail of the wonderfully worn wooden print block.

below A collage of old and new maps makes a recycled version of wallpaper.

recycling

We all know that we should recycle as much as we can, carefully separating jam jars from cereal packets and newspapers. In the same way, reconsider how you shop for furniture; it's time to rescue, re-think and reuse – visit flea markets, bazaars, antique fairs and reclamation yards. People throw too much stuff away, so encourage an end to this culture of disposability. Other people's junk could be your perfect table, chair, piece of storage and so forth.

Have an open mind and don't stop searching until you find something to fall instantly in love with. It's probably not going to be about the task you need them to perform in your home; it's more likely to be down to texture, a flash of bright colour peeking out from layers of flaky paint or the signs of quality craftsmanship. If you're prepared to think differently about what goes where, then any piece of furniture has a role to play in all the rooms of your house.

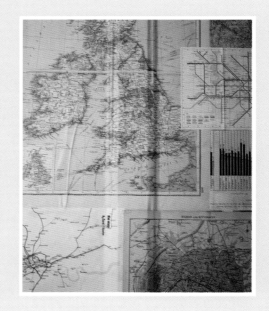

below A stripey patchwork blanket made from strips of suiting fabric is used to cover the blemishes of an old chair.

right A jacket made from military canvas kitbags.

It goes without saying that old furniture will have flaws, blemishes and imperfections, especially if you find something hidden under piles of junk at a flea market. These signs of wear and tear should be seen as qualities – proof of age and individuality; characteristics you're not going to find in mass-produced, flat-packed convenience furniture. Take the trouble to repair if necessary, but don't fuss with invisible mending. If you find a comfy looking chair with worn-out upholstery,

throw on some vintage fabric cushions, or a handcrafted patchwork blanket. In this way, you hide the small imperfections and create the perfect place to curl up with a mug of coffee and a good book. Don't be fooled by appearances – give outdoor furniture a treat and use it inside your home instead; it will thank you for it! A weathered garden bench makes ideal seating alongside a chunky wooden kitchen table, and if you need extra seating, a curly ironwork chair provides decorative contrast too. Don't be afraid to mix old and new; worn, faded furniture looks even better next to a sleek, shiny stainless steel

DELIBERATELY MISMATCHING GIVES YOUR HOME INDIVIDUALITY AND A MORE RELAXED ELEGANCE.

oven or fridge, or when it's providing a resting place for an up-to-the-minute television or music player. Be creative; even a worn-out old door has its uses – try it as an unusual shelf. If you have a collection of postcards hidden away, old wooden rulers make amazing skinny shelving that is perfect for showing them off. Pieces of floorboard and architrave make beautiful patchwork frames for mirrors or paintings, or tabletops. Surprise yourself by turning an old

French brioche tin or jelly mould into an unusual lampshade – just get someone who knows what they're doing with electricity to help you! The list is endless once you have thrown out pre-conceived ideas and learned to see the potential in absolutely everything.

The simple home is not about feeling stressed out because you can't find the right set of dining chairs or cutlery. Deliberately mismatching gives your home individuality and a more relaxed form

top left Take a closer look – an old door has been put to good use here as an elevated shelf for well-read novels.

centre Two creative examples of recycling – an oversized galvanized catering colander and an old brioche tin have been turned into ingenious and interestingly shaped light shades.

below A decorator's trestle table has been brought into the home and makes a surprisingly elegant dining table, especially when accompanied by a station waiting-room bench.

opposite Reconsidering how you use things creates an element of surprise in your home, as shown here by a row of wooden-spoon hooks.

SIMPLICITY IS THE WATCHWORD HERE – DON'T FILL YOUR HOME WITH TOO MANY THINGS, AS IT CAN QUICKLY DESCEND INTO CLUTTER.

of elegance – pick things that you really, really love; not just because they go with the other five chairs parked around your table or forks nestling in your kitchen drawers.

An added bonus to furniture recycling is that it means you don't have to be too precious about your furniture finds. They've already aged pretty well, and with just a little bit of cleaning, care and attention from you, they'll keep on growing old gracefully, whatever you or your family throws at them.

Do be choosy when perusing flea and antique markets or even the internet – there are lots of good websites out there selling vintage furniture. Remember that simplicity is the watchword here. Don't fill your home with too many things, as it can quickly become overwhelming and descend into clutter. Recycled finds need space in order to fully show off their beautiful imperfections. One or two well-considered larger items provide an unusual talking point, while smaller finds, such as kitchenware, storage jars, old suitcases or stationery, do their jobs with quiet, understated elegance.

comfort

opposite One huge sofa covered in loose linen sits opposite a Chesterfield that is covered unusually in dark linen. The reassuringly sturdy stone fireplace, complete with a log-burning stove and Cornish granite floor, give the room a comfortingly timeless quality.

above left Generous amounts of daylight are allowed into this room by the parting of a pair of simple linen curtains.

above right An inviting pair of squashy, feather-filled cushions in contrasting fabrics.

Your home should be a serene and tranquil domestic landscape in which to sit back and relax, giving you the chance to forget the stresses of the day. The kind of comfort you seek ultimately depends on the season, but whatever the time of year, you can't go wrong with a huge, squashy sofa piled high with plump cushions – then it's up to you and the elements as to whether or not you light the fire.

The components that make up the look of the simple home – colours, materials, handicraft and recycling – all add up to a comfortable, happy habitat. Be sure to throw them all into the mix, otherwise your home could end up hard-edged, overly minimal and off-puttingly austere.

below An assortment of cushions of varying textures, shapes and sizes invites you to curl up on this sofa. The heavily textured knitted cushions lend a cosy feel, while the others add pattern and colour.

inset Patches of bright neon orange embroidery provide a vivid flash of contrasting colour on this cushion covered in an old linen tea towel.

opposite A few crumples add to the textural values of the easy, elegant home.

The natural materials that predominate in both the structure and furniture in your home – stone, wood and raw brickwork – bring the outside in. They remind us of ruddy-cheeked walks in the country, happily trudging through golden autumn leaves, knowing that a fireside Sunday lunch isn't far away. They're like super-sized versions of the small treasures you might collect on one of these idyllic rambles – skinny twigs, shiny conkers, feathers and pebbles. They are instilled with memories that make us feel warm and ready to hibernate on less clement days, when the rain beats against the windows.

right Soft folds of lightweight fabric wrapped around a bed piled with pillows create a cosy comfort zone in this compact Parisian apartment.

opposite top left Extra-large stitching gives a reassuringly handcrafted feel to this chunky sofa. The roughly woven tapestry behind brings another warm, textural dimension.

opposite centre A pile of Egyptian cotton-filled floor cushions, covered in mousy-coloured linens creates an impromptu resting spot.

opposite top right Shelves of simply decorated, handwoven Indian cotton.

opposite below Everything about the creative process of this beautiful handwoven Indian linen with tribal embroidery speaks of serene simplicity; from the planting of the cotton to spinning it by hand into an uneven yarn.

The milky-soft, natural colours in your home are reminiscent of large mugs of hot chocolate and add to the feeling of relaxation. Make sure that you use paint with a matt finish, as it has a velvety feel, and avoid glaringly shiny plastics, which are more in keeping with the sterile look of a doctor's waiting room. A rich mix of contrasting textures adds to the comforting mood.

Use expanses of easy-to-find utilitarian fabrics such as ticking or canvas to cover your sofa or as a hard-working tablecloth. Add richer, velvety fabrics and a few vintage textiles, softened over time and washing cycles. As with recycled furniture, a flea-market find of well-loved vintage fabrics that have been cared for over the years will give you a warm, cosy glow. As long as they're fresh, a few frayed edges here and there won't matter at all – in fact, they lend an air of relaxed grandeur. Then place your texture-rich sofas and chairs around the fireplace, making it the heart of your living room rather than the television, light a fire and snuggle up under a chunky hand-knitted blanket. All you need to complete the picture is a cup of tea and maybe a gently purring cat. Meeeow!

natural cleaning

above left A waffle-textured cloth and a well-crafted wooden nail brush are ready to hand, resting on an old wall tap.

above right A wooden-handled bristle broom rests against the wall after a hard time sweeping this beautiful hardwood floor. Its utilitarian nature is effectively contrasted with the delicately carved chaise.

opposite An array of wiry bottle brushes are stored in vintage milk bottles. There is one for every occasion and shape of bottle.

If your house is clean and tidy, it's a sign that you treat it with the respect it deserves. A spick and span house is also the perfect foil for the graceful imperfections of the natural materials that make up your home. There's no denying that cleaning is a constant chore, but it can be less painful and better for the environment if you make your own cleaning products. It feels good to be safe in the knowledge that there's nothing with too high a chemical content in your cleaning cupboard. Use beautiful tools too; it's much more pleasing to employ a well-constructed beechwood brush with soft horsehair bristles or an ostrich feather duster, and makes cleaning feel almost glamorous.

BEESWAX POLISH

Beeswax polish is the very best choice for keeping wood looking good, or for perking up any tired wooden furniture. All you need to make your own creamy polish are equal amounts of turpentine and beeswax – and a wide-mouthed jam jar with a lid. If you have a favourite essential oil, you could also add a few drops to the polish.

Get in touch with your local beekeepers' association for advice on buying beeswax. Turpentine should be available from good art shops or hardware stores – make sure you get the real thing, not turps substitute.

The absolutely simplest way to make it is to combine the two ingredients in the jam jar, screw on the lid and leave it in a warm place for a few days. Eventually the beeswax will dissolve in the turpentine.

If you're in more of a hurry to get polishing, you can speed up the process by melting the beeswax first. If you do, be extremely careful. Melt the wax the way you would melt chocolate – by setting the container of wax over a saucepan of hot water. Have a damp tea towel to hand in case disaster strikes.

Apply the finished polish with a cloth or soft brush, leave for about 20 minutes, then polish with a soft cloth – you don't need to use much so it should last a while.

left Beeswax is easily made at home and is the most superb polish possible for bringing out the best in wood.

below An ostrich feather duster hangs out with a variety of wire food covers and trays and an industrially huge colander. Its signs of wear and tear are proof of its fine cleaning pedigree.

To clean well, cheaply and safely throughout the home, all you need are the recipes included here and some basic ingredients – distilled white vinegar, bicarbonate of soda (baking soda) and lemons. Those and a little bit of elbow grease should go a long way. It's also worth reusing items such as old toothbrushes to clean hard-to-reach corners and squares of old cotton t-shirts or sheets as dusters. Just remember to wash or boil them regularly and you need never buy another duster again.

Distilled white vinegar has a myriad of cleaning uses, as well as being an effective disinfectant and deodorizer. It is safe to use on most surfaces (apart from marble) and is incredibly cheap. Use it in the bathroom to clean the bath, shower, toilet, sink and taps. To

From left to right – a vintage banister brush, a goat-hair dusting brush with extra soft bristles for delicate dusting, horsehair brush, a sturdy stainless steel dustpan, a vintage cornice brush, an old banister brush for reaching dizzy heights, a sculptural-style behind-the-cupboard brush and an ostrich feathered duster.

FURNITURE POLISH

This is perfect for everyday cleaning, and is handily made from simple storecupboard ingredients.

Mix together the juice of one lemon with a teaspoon of olive oil (ordinary olive oil is best here; save the fancy extra-virgin variety for salads) and a teaspoon of water. The lemon cuts through any greasy grime and smells deliciously fresh; the olive oil conditions and polishes the wood.

This polish needs to be made fresh every time.

get rid of limescale deposits around a shower head, fill a bowl with hot vinegar heated in a saucepan and immerse the shower head for no longer than an hour, then scrub off the loose limescale with an old toothbrush. Run the shower to remove any excess vinegar.

To remove limescale from taps, wrap paper towels around the base of the taps where it usually gathers, then pour hot vinegar onto the paper towel sheets until saturated. Again, leave for about an hour, then rinse thoroughly and buff to a shine. Vinegar also

LINEN WATER

Going to sleep in freshly laundered sheets is one of life's simple pleasures and can be made even more luxurious if you've used softly scented linen water. It's easy to make and you can add your favourite essential oil to sweeten your dreams.

You will need 90ml high-proof vodka (80+ is best and make sure that it's not flavoured), 750ml distilled water (totally pure water, available from most grocery or hardware stores) and a teaspoon of essential oil (lavender is often used and is said to aid a good night's sleep).

Pour the ingredients into a clean, dry glass or plastic bottle, ideally one with a spray top. Close the bottle and shake to mix the oil and alcohol (the vodka emulsifies the oil to give an evenly mixed solution). Shake well before each use.

works wonders in the kitchen – use it to clean all work surfaces and appliances. As well as having cleaning power, vinegar can also eliminate lingering cooking odours – simply simmer a solution of vinegar and water in a pan for five minutes. For gleaming windows, mix one part vinegar with three parts warm water. Dunk an old cotton tea towel in the solution and rub on the windows before using some scrunched newspaper to buff them.

above A tiny pair of antique embroidery scissors hangs above piles of freshly folded crisp white linen.

left Simple stripey linen tea towels hang from a row of 'S' hooks, ready for action.

opposite Linen water can be made at home from a surprising storecupboard ingredient – vodka (well it might be in your cupboard if it's your favourite tipple)! Once you have blended the basic constituents, add your favourite essential oil to lightly scent your ironing.

Use bicarbonate of soda (baking soda) in the bathroom and kitchen. Put it on a damp cloth to clean all surface types and use for cleaning the oven – make a paste with equal parts salt, bicarbonate of soda and water, paste onto oven walls and leave for a while (preferably overnight), then wipe off. It also works well as a deodorizer; place a box in the fridge to absorb odours.

Finally, lemon juice is a multi-tasking miracle worker too. Use it in the recipe for furniture polish or mix with bicarbonate of soda to make a cleaning paste for all manner of surfaces.

By keeping things natural, you'll cut back on costs and waste, and reduce the number of harsh chemicals at work in your home.

this page These sturdy wooden chairs double as casual tables holding treasure-filled lacquered deed boxes. The white wood-panelled wall feels contrastingly clean and fresh.

opposite above Chunky colonial-looking chairs sit at the end of the bed. Their solid frames have an air of Bauhaus angularity about them.

opposite below A couple of handcrafted bamboo chairs sit side by side in a roughly hewn hallway.

Furniture makes your home work; it can offer a place to sit, eat, sleep, work or rest, but also does all manner of other important jobs too – like hiding washing powder and looking after your books. A well-chosen collection of furniture adds colour and detail to your home, provides textural contrast or complements what you already have in place on your walls and floors.

Recycled furniture from salvage yards, antique shops and flea markets is usually the most sympathetic to the simple home style. Make sure everything is in working order, or at least nothing that a few minor repairs can't fix.

Remember to keep an open mind about what you can use where and be choosy; you don't want to overstuff your attempted shrine to simplicity. It's a good idea to choose furniture that allows plenty of light to flood around it – it fits in with the mildly minimal ethos of simple style and it goes for all your furniture, from leggy metal bar stools to glass-fronted medical cabinets mounted on long limbs.

furniture

CHAIRS ARE THE SOCIAL ANIMALS OF THE FURNITURE WORLD, SO PLACE THEM IN FRIENDLY GROUPS. THEY DON'T HAVE TO MATCH IN ORDER TO GET ON WELL.

Alternatively, team up chunkier items with skinnier friends, as their contrasting characteristics create the perfect match. The same goes if you come across a must-have item that is a little more elaborate – make it a talking point by leaving everything else plain. If your decorative find is a little bit battered around the edges, then leave it this way as it will ooze timeless elegance much more so than a shiny, repaired version of its former self.

Tables are where people gather for mealtimes, to read the papers or just to chat over a pot of fresh coffee, so seek out the largest one you can fit in your space. Choose sturdy tables that have seen some action and are up to the rigours of daily life, be they overenthusiastic finger painting or red wine spillages; you don't want to be constantly worrying about perfect polishing. If you can't find one big enough, then get two and join them together; it really doesn't matter if they don't match. Long wooden refectory tables are timeless classics and look great. If legs are a little wobbly, replace them with contrasting skinny metal ones. Circular café tables or tables rescued from the garden are well worth considering if you're short on space.

Chairs are the social animals of the furniture world, so place them in friendly groups. Again, they don't have to match; all manner of different chairs get on marvellously. Look out for chairs that are keen to show off just how comfortable they are. Slightly worn seats and arms are sure

above A myriad of different textures are at work here, with a glass-fronted cabinet of curiosities perched on a chest made from rescued wooden boards and a block of wood acting as a simple low table.

this page A trio of mismatched antique chairs are connected by their plain linen upholstery. The decorative nature of the turned double seat and traditional gateleg table are balanced by the huge inglenook fireplace.

opposite Don't neglect shelving! A wooden trolley on wheels rescued from a shoe factory clearance sale neatly stores recycled cardboard boxes of paperwork and files.

left A set of shelves brought in from the cold of the potting shed holds a collection of glass cake plates. Its rough edges and flaky paint highlight the fragility of the glass.

above right An Indian shelving unit formerly used to hold jars has come to rest in the nursery, holding recycled cardboard wastepaper bins, which in turn store a zoo full of brightly coloured toy animals.

right A metal-framed factory trolley makes excellent kitchen storage. Every aspect has been used, with the addition of hooks to hold an oven glove.

signs that someone once thought they were good to sit in – over and over again! Take a seat and try it for size before finally deciding it's the one for you – even if it needs a lick of paint or a slim cushion to hide less attractive comfy credentials. Canvas or stripey ticking are perfect fabrics for covering chairs that need a bit of attention, as they are more than up to the wear and tear of family life and are also ideal for making heavy-duty, hard-wearing cushion covers. Chairs with a variety of past lives come alive once more when invited into your home. Wooden church pews, chapel chairs and garden benches are great for parking a number of people around your kitchen table. Cinema seats, café chairs or

wooden lab stools all have a part to play too. Don't forget about the classics either – if you're lucky enough to find some 1950s gems such as a skeletal Antelope chair by Ernest Race or a wiry Bertoia chair, made by Harry Bertoia for Knoll then snap it up without a second thought.

Sofas are an extremely important investment purchase and worth spending a little bit extra on if you can. The unofficial rule of thumb with a sofa has to be to buy one that you can stretch out on and that will accommodate you and your friends for an afternoon of classic film watching. You'll also need cushions to hide behind and a coffee table close to hand – though it doesn't

this page Soft geometric shapes in the form of a silvered leather pouf and a metal-framed daybed offer informal seating options in this pale but interesting corner.

opposite Classic chairs work well in all situations. Here, a wiry Bertoia chair sits with a similarly leggy friend around a table piled with treasures, all reflected in an 18th-century French mirror and lit by a bare bulb suspended from a long, knotted cord.

this page An extra-long table with a beautifully scuffed painted surface stands elegantly in a sunny kitchen. A pair of simple wooden benches provides ample seating for hungry hoards.

above A chunky stainless steel surface with integral hob has been cleverly engineered to suspend from the steel ceiling prop. This makes the most of the available space and emphasizes the industrial style of the rescued factory chairs.

right A scrubbed wooden top on curvy steel legs gives a sculptural twist to this informal dining table, and reflects the graphic nature of the extra-large steel Crittal window.

necessarily have to be a table; an old tin trunk provides the perfect perch for a Brown Betty teapot and a plate stacked with chocolate cookies. It's probably wise to go for a brand new sofa; there are so many well-crafted slouchy sofas out there and really old ones might poke you in the behind with a sharp spring while you're perusing the Sunday papers! However, leather sofas do age gracefully and lend an air of old-school sophistication and charm to your home. If you find one that fits the bill but is a little too well worn in places, then throw on a cosy blanket to hide the more significant blemishes.

Shelves are often an afterthought when hunting for furniture, which is a shame as they offer so much. Redundant factory

A WELL-CHOSEN COLLECTION OF FURNITURE ADDS COLOUR AND DETAIL TO YOUR HOME, AS WELL AS PROVIDING TEXTURAL CONTRAST.

rejects are a good place to start if you can track one down. Their slightly bashed wooden frames are ideal for all the rooms in your house. They'll hold everything, from neatly labelled boxes of stationery in your home office to wonky piles of plates and glasses in your kitchen or a host of stuffed toys in the nursery. Even better news is that they're usually set on wheels, making them even more flexible. For fixed shelves, get a friendly carpenter to make you some bespoke ones out of abandoned pieces of wood; weathered railway sleepers or old reclaimed floorboards are ideal for this job. If you want to close the door on your piles of paperwork or eco-friendly canvas shopper collection (you know you've got one), then freestanding cupboards are the answer. Don't feel restricted by their previous employment. Formerly glamorous wardrobes and armoires take on the challenge of kitchen storage. Sturdy wooden beasts previously used as storage for hammers and nails, covered in all manner of historical paint splodges and splashes, look at ease in more elegant surroundings.

above left This sturdy glazed dresser from the 1800s was discovered in an antique shop in Provence. It provides ample storage space in its many drawers, while the faded charm and original blue paintwork easily stands up to the grandeur of the carved marble fireplace.

above right An old decorative 1800s French armoire has a lovely feeling of faded elegance with its original, worn painted surface. The linen loose cover on the chair and lightly creased tablecloth add to the relaxed atmosphere of the room.

this page It seems someone started to cover up the beautiful worn wooden surface of this curved cupboard with paint before realizing the error of their ways. The shell-like shapes of the decorative ceramics are reflected in the well-chosen line drawing hanging above.

this page Your private gallery space can be anywhere in your home. Here, a stairwell has been used to house a collection of unusual found objects. The scuffed tiles and weathered wooden board are in stark contrast to the white steps and grey cushions, but the matching tonal values keep a balance.

opposite left Extra-long simple stems lined up in a mismatched collection of old lemonade bottles make a feature of an open-plan staircase.

opposite right Wooden print block, an oversized atlas and the bold silhouette of an old office fan share a strong graphic theme. A Michelin man figure watches the world go by.

curating your home

Curating collections of art, found objects or cherished travel mementos is the fun part of creating the simple home – to live simply doesn't mean that you can't build up a vast collection of your favourite things. What you have to do is think of yourself as a museum or art gallery curator and your home as your very own personal museum. In this way, your prized possessions remain a constant source of delight rather than degenerating into mere piles of clutter. In the real world of museums and galleries, the curator is responsible for the acquisition and care of objects. When adopting this role in the home, the same applies. Happily, what you have in your personal collection or how you acquire it is less restrictive than it is for actual museums. Just about anything can become a collection; it could be triggered by coming across a beautiful object in a junk store and deciding to collect other similar things.

You could decide to turn your one or two postcards into a more substantial assortment. Wooden print block, old tins or other quirky examples of vintage packaging, play-worn toys or even typewriters could be the obsession for you. Found objects, bits of weathered wood, feathers, even fragments of animal skull collected on walks in the country or seashells amassed on family holidays make lovely displays and are imbued with memories of special moments; they match the natural warmth of the materials in the simple home, and what's more they're free! Look around – you may already have a collection without even realizing it. All it takes is to sort your items into some kind of theme.

this page Putting unexpected items together can create a surprisingly eloquent still life. Here, the fragility of the dried leaf emphasizes the timeless elegance of this collection of antique silverware.

opposite A lovely little booklet on moths and butterflies by artist John Dilnot accompanies the pressed ferns perfectly.

Coming up with a strategy for your display is another hugely important part of the curator's job description. In the home it elevates your potentially disparate array of goodies into something special. Decide on a theme and stick to it, but not forever or things could get a bit tired; people wouldn't keep returning to the Tate gallery if the display never changed. Take a good look at what you've got; consider texture, colour, materials, matching content or anything that works for you and your particular collection.

far left A collection of oddly shaped ceramic pots, vases and vessels sit comfortably with piles of well-read paperbacks. Whether by design or good luck the ensemble works very well, creating a perfectly colour-matched assembly.

left Unusual jugs of all shapes and sizes, including one with an unusual glaze that has the look of wet clay, are displayed on plain wooden shelves, with informally leaning black and white prints and photographs. The unexpected addition of a large spring adds an extra linear quality, which reflects both the subjects and style of the artworks.

above right A cupboard lined with a quirky collection of man-made versions of nature – lettuce leaves and oysters. Shells add warmth to these unexpected small treasures.

below right A black and white collection of wobbly piles of kitchenware, graphic pictures, postcards and a McDougalls flour man are thoughtfully arranged on a skinny steel shelf and a rescued factory trolley.

Once you have a theme, the next step is how to show off your assortment. This can be another way of bringing your collection together, as well as keeping the dust off. If you display objects in a row of glass domes, cloches or even glass cake covers, it brings a sense of unity, no matter how incongruent your items are.

this page An interesting array of objects congregate on this table – insect drawings, votive candles, a broken Hector lamp, a wise-looking plaster bust and an iPod, all surveyed by a man peering from a dark painting.

opposite above left A collection of old wooden shoe lasts paraded on metal shelves.

opposite above centre Frames of pressed seaweed and leaves hang on a rough wall with a similar texture to lichen.

opposite above right Various misty Victorian mirrors gently reflect light, while guarded by a pair of beautifully carved wings.

opposite below left A travel theme is created by the pile of old trunks and a London Routemaster bus blind. A reused brioche tin makes a lampshade, while a hanging chair awaits guests.

opposite below right Old food larders and safes store toys. Printed cushions sit on a slatted wooden seat from a 1950s bus.

this page The glass domes, framed seaweed and a brown apothecary bottle bring a scientific feel to this table of strange treasures. The overall whiteness of the display adds to the clinical effect but this is ultimately softened by a pile of old black and white postcards and fluted ceramic dishes.

Glass-fronted medicine cabinets are perfect for the job – they keep everything together, thus denying the descent into clutter, and are usually lockable, giving the collection a certain mystery – turning mundane objects into a Renaissance-style cabinet of curiosities. Keep an eye out for glazed wooden boxes too; they are very museum-like and give you the opportunity to turn your everyday bits and pieces into magical, mini works of art in the manner of the American surrealist Joseph Cornell. The items you put next to each other under your domes or in your display cupboards or glass-covered boxes are all important. This is curating as alchemy – two objects arranged next to each other magicially transform both and create a third thing – which has the power to trigger cascades of thought and reaction.

Collections of art or photos don't always have to be framed and hung on your walls. You can create a more relaxed feel by casually leaning small groups of them against your walls instead, either on a tabletop or on the floor. If you find a piece of art that you like but

BY KEEPING YOUR DISPLAYS WELL CONSIDERED, YOU WILL HAVE MORE BREATHING SPACE AND IT WILL MAKE YOUR ROLE AS CURATOR ALL THE MORE CHALLENGING.

in a frame that you don't, simply free it from the offending frame and mount it on a piece of cut-to-size plywood instead or suspend it from small, shiny bulldog clips and string. If you do decide to hang them suitably framed on your wall, then go for small, dynamic groups, with images playing off against each other.

Something to keep in mind, especially in view of the clutter-free ideals of the simple home, is that at any given time museums display only a small portion of their collection. You don't have to show everything off at once. By keeping your displays well considered, you will have more space and it will make your role as

Various silver-plated hotel dishes crowd together on a vintage Hungarian linen table runner. Their shininess contrasts well with the chunky black stone bowls from India. In the alcove sit three mercury glass vases. The delicate wall hanging is made from thin pieces of porcelain.

A scattering of silver-plated
hotel ware gives the sense that
this kitchen shelf holds untold
treasures – it does in fact
include a vintage soda siphon
and cocktail shaker.

WHAT YOU HAVE TO DO IS TO THINK OF YOURSELF AS A MUSEUM OR ART GALLERY CURATOR AND SEE YOUR HOME AS YOUR VERY OWN PERSONAL MUSEUM.

opposite far left Circuit boards mounted onto a panel become an artwork in their own right. When seen like this, the intricate detail that goes into them can be appreciated. Its elevation into the art world is emphasized by the framed drawings and paintings leaning next to a shapely wooden chair.

opposite top right A vintage tailor's dummy creates a still life while it works. Piled next to it is a collection of old cotton shirts.

opposite below far left A vintage globe sits on an unusual turned wooden base.

opposite below centre An old theatre spotlight is poised to flood a late night game of table soccer with light.

opposite below right A close-up view of the game in action.

curator all the more challenging. Safely store away some of your cherished collection in boxes, corrugated paper or tissue. If you are worried about aging, use acid-free tissue or clear archival holders, available from specialist art shops. Then you can rotate and change your displays as and when you feel like it, which will keep the rooms in your home fresh. Once you have adopted this innovative idea there's endless fun to be had, but whatever you decide, it's always a good plan to introduce the odd unexpected element to give a sense of fun and keep people looking.

Ultimately, lots of the more mundane everyday things can become a less precious kind of collection if they've been well designed and most things look good in quantity. Look out for nicely packaged groceries and store them on open shelving in a way that turns them into still lifes from every angle. Or, if the packaging isn't up to much, then decant into glass storage jars. Rather than alphabetizing your books, rearrange them into waves of colour. Whatever makes you happy – it's your museum!

above left A themed collection of star shapes.

above centre The tagua beads and polished seed heads give this mirror a soft, feathery feel.

above right Print block spells out the all-important theme!

spaces

We all want to make a good impression, and that goes for your home as well. Wading through piles of newspapers and mounds of unwanted junk mail waiting to be recycled is not going to put your home in a good light with visitors, neither is tripping over discarded shoes and boots.

For an inviting entrance and clear hallway, all it takes is some care, organization and considered storage. Hooks keep hats, coats, scarves and bags out of the way and off the floor. They don't have to be conventional – there are all sorts of quirky hooks out there. But get creative; all manner of things could work if you're feeling a little bit experimental. Try a row of wooden spoons or thick twigs. Alternatively, a curvy classic Café Daum coat stand,

above This busy entrance brings you straight into the heart of a hard-working kitchen. Baskets stand ready for more fruit and veg collecting.

below left Glass panels in the front door allow light to flood this narrow hallway. A white floor adds to the sunny feel.

below right The walls in this entrance have been painted in gradients of soft grey, which give a feeling of light flowing into the furthest reaches of the space. The geometric lines add to the graphic feel of the tiles.

opposite Panels of sheer fabric suspended from cables add softness to this narrow entrance with its solid stone floor. An industrial wall light adds to the contrast of textures.

entrances & hallways

designed by Michael Thonet, solved the 'where to put my coat' dilemma for Viennese café society, so why not let it do the same for you? If there's space, fit a narrow shelf for keys and all those other things you can never find when you're in a hurry. If you are lucky enough to have a little extra space, then a skinny chair is a treat for putting on shoes. A blackboard in your hallway or on the landing between rooms is the ideal way to get important reminders and messages across.

Entrances and hallways should ideally be light-filled spaces, and obviously glass-fronted doorways are a great idea as long as safety or laminated glass is used. But a small amount of glass goes a long way in a slim entrance hall, and if you are worried about nosy neighbours, choose a piece of etched or opaque glass; it can become a subtly decorative feature if you get it right. Sticking to a fairly monochrome palette can help to make entrances and hallways seem larger (in the same way as wearing the same colour shoes as your tights can create the impression of longer legs!). Painting the floors and walls in a pale, light-reflecting shade makes them almost seamless.

above Contrasting white wooden boards lead down to a natural-coloured hallway; the balustrading has Shaker-style hearts cut out of it. A skeletally framed chair is a handy spot for tying shoelaces.

below left Beautiful sawn wooden boards follow the curves of the staircase, leading you up the stairs as they wind around the corner.

below right Stairs worn down the middle through years of use. Their sturdiness contrasts with the delicate wall embroidery.

this page The family dog guards the landing (though he doesn't appear to be too ferocious). The addition of a blackboard provides the perfect spot for leaving messages, as well as cute drawings of birds. A collection of glass vases filled with pebbles and shells are reminders of holidays spent joyfully beachcombing.

this page A series of interconnecting rooms in this French apartment shows the different functions of floors, as you step from roughly hewn stone flooring through to glazed floor tiles.

If you're lucky enough to have inherited beautiful Victorian floor tiles in your entrance hall, don't even think about getting rid of them, even though they may feel too vivid for a simple interior. If you keep everything else as plain and tidy as possible, these tiles will help create the perfect first impression of your home, as well as being true to its history. Victorian floor tiles are usually made from pretty robust ceramic, but may be suffering from hundreds of years of wear and tear. If this is the case, unfortunately it will take a bit of elbow grease to clean them. Avoid harsh chemicals that will add to their worn feel and plump for a natural cleaner with bicarbonate of soda (baking soda) or distilled white vinegar as a base instead. Don't get the tiles too wet and scrub them with the kind of non-scratch scourers you would use on your best pans. For further tips and recipes, refer to the natural cleaning chapter.

STICKING TO A FAIRLY MONOCHROME PALETTE CAN MAKE ENTRANCES AND HALLWAYS SEEM MORE SPACIOUS.

above right Smooth white floors sweep you seamlessly from room to room. The lower half of the corridor walls are painted black to match the monochrome kitchen.

below left Beautiful French parquet flooring with its classic herringbone pattern is a fine feature in this Parisian flat, belonging to architects Anki Linde and Pierre Saalburg.

below right Bert the cat peeks out from behind the laundry room door. The sanded floor helps lighten a dark hallway.

cooking & eating

opposite An ample, nearly floor-to-ceiling dresser provides generous storage for cream-ware jugs, plain white plates, wobbly carafes and café-style glasses. The table shows off its age with a surface worn smooth over the years. A row of hand-printed polar bear tags strung above the table adds humour.

above left Old rescued floor tiles act as a splashback and provide a battered contrast to the sleek mixer tap.

above right Shelves are given some colour with gingham linen.

As the whole house becomes less and less compartmentalized, the recent trend for combining kitchens and dining rooms makes perfect sense, as it results in much more versatile, casual spaces for cooking and eating. This way, the member of the family providing the evening meal doesn't feel cut off from the fun going on in the rest of the house and cooking becomes more of a sociable leisure activity. With the aid of a kitchen island, the chef can take centre stage while cooking and entertaining. As well as that, it's a much more practical design solution, as the food can quickly go from stove to tabletop and arrive piping hot without the need for an awful 1970s-style hostess trolley.

TAPS SHOULDN'T BE OVERLOOKED – GO FOR ONES THAT YOU MIGHT FIND IN A PROFESSIONAL KITCHEN, THAT YOU CAN EASILY TURN ON AND OFF.

Before the cooking, eating, working, playing or whatever else you think might happen in your space starts, plenty of consideration needs to go into the planning stage. This is certainly one area of the house that demands any extra cash to be lavished on one or two essential appliances. Indulge yourself in the biggest and best oven you can afford and fit into your kitchen; go for something rugged and industrial so that it becomes a long-term investment that will stand up to the demands you put on it. The same goes for the fridge – the roomier the better and a shiny stainless steel or pale pastel American-style one won't need to be slyly hidden away behind a false door. Taps shouldn't be overlooked either. Again, go for ones that you might find in a professional kitchen; those that you can easily turn on and off, even when your hands are covered in flour or sticky clumps of pastry. Ones with an extendable hose attachment make washing up after a big meal or pre-dishwasher rinsing easier to deal with too.

Expensively fitted kitchens that are more of a status symbol than an actual place to work are definitely not what is required in the simple home. Once your cooker and fridge are in place (and

this page Space is at a premium in this apartment, but the owners, architects Anki Linde and Pierre Saalburg, have come up with the ideal solution – a cantilevered brushed aluminium work surface, which extends into a useful dining and workspace. This ingenious space saver also provides shelter for a Smeg oven and a gang of six contrastingly classic French stools designed by Xavier Pauchard in 1934.

opposite Brushed aluminium adds a surprising softness to this efficiently designed kitchen.

this page This light and airy kitchen space boasts surprising contrasting details. The smooth, olive green cupboards, shiny oven and sleek marble surface are offset by a flakily painted wall cupboard and wide, unfinished floorboards. If you should look upwards, the intricate cornicing has been left undisturbed by paint.

KITCHEN ISLANDS ALLOW THE HARD-WORKING COOK TO KEEP CHOPPING WITHOUT TURNING THEIR BACK ON VISITORS.

above left Split bamboo provides the backdrop to this utilitarian space, which is filled with an array of shiny steel tea urns, teapots and an industrial coffee machine. Just the thing for shots of dark espresso, drunk leaning against the extra-thick, wooden tabletop.

above right The contrastingly rustic detail of the bamboo is shown in detail here.

be sure to work out exactly where the very best place is) freestanding cupboards, old wooden dressers and open shelves are the eye-pleasing, natural alternative. They allow you to mix and match as you wish and give a much more pared-down feel to your kitchen rather than the often sterile, over-designed feel of its uptight fitted cousin. Kitchen islands are increasingly popular too, as they mean that the hard-working cook doesn't have to turn their back on visitors while they chop away. Ignore convention and look out for extra-large cupboards or chests of

drawers to act as your island. Not only will you (or your sous chef) be able to face the hungry audience, but there will also be some sneaky extra storage into the bargain for all those rarely used kitchen gadgets.

It is almost impossible to have a minimalist approach to your cooking space – unless you want to become a very familiar face at your local restaurant or spend all hours cleaning. However, this doesn't mean that the ideals of the simple home can be ignored altogether. Far from it – there are plenty of opportunities to employ natural materials that will add to the overall warmth of the space. These come in the guise of tables, chairs and one-off pieces of furniture, as well as old wooden chopping boards and spoons. Again, it's best to decorate with low-key, milky colours. Anything brighter might put you off your food! The simple pale colour palette sits quietly in the background, feels wonderfully fresh and allows light to reflect off its surface, flooding your kitchen and dining space with all-important natural light. A lick of well-chosen eggshell paint can work wonders and harmonize the desired look. Or alternatively, take a complete about-turn and scrape off all the paint, then polish the plasterwork for the ultimate in simple style; just keep textures matt everywhere except for your sleek, shiny cooker.

After the oven and fridge, the table is probably the hardest-working element of your cooking and eating space. Think of all the activities that are likely to take place around the kitchen table – you'll quickly come to the conclusion that it is much more than a place for mealtimes. So the bigger the table you can find and have space for, the better. Wouldn't it be

above A skylight illuminates this space dominated by honey-toned wood. An artwork by Julian Stair's father, Bill Stair gives textural contrast while ceramics by Julian and Richard Batterham sit on the shelf.

left Slim shelves are a great way to make room for storage.

wonderful if your table was long enough to push half-finished crosswords, homework, pens and piles of books to one end, allowing you to dine at the other without feeling overwhelmed? Chunky wooden refectory tables are perfect for this particular role, as are long tables with drawers, which provide essential extra storage. Lovely weathered wooden tables such as these age well and don't need constant polishing – just the occasional rub with some homemade beeswax polish. They can stand up to the challenge of hot pans or poster paint-covered fingers and give you extra food preparation space too. Long benches mixed up with industrial steel stools and curly but slightly rusty garden chairs are the perfect seating partners for such charmingly rugged tables.

THE RECENT TREND FOR COMBINING KITCHENS AND DINING ROOMS RESULTS IN A MUCH MORE VERSATILE CASUAL SPACE FOR COOKING AND EATING.

below left A vast kitchen island allows the chef to take centre stage, while a pair of roughly edged slate roof tiles act as a splashback and a handy message board.

below right A collection of beautiful textured teapots nestle on a grainy wooden shelf.

If space doesn't allow for never-endingly long tables, then look to your favourite café for inspiration. High stools around an extended counter give your kitchen area a more industrial edge and can be the ideal solution to a lack of space. They may also get you even closer to the cooking action (though if this is the case, be prepared to lend a helping hand).

If you inherit your kitchen long after the planning stage, when it's too late or just not the right time for major structural changes

or refits, it's good to remember that little changes can make all the difference. Think of ways that you can add extra storage including, if possible, open-plan shelving for your more loved kitchen bits and pieces. Cooking and eating spaces are another place where you can indulge a passion for collecting, and in this case the collection has a purpose too. These kitchen collections could range from teapots or jugs to stacks of wobbly white crockery (the quirky French design duo Tsé & Tsé create beautiful,

this page An enormous cantilevered stainless-steel surface, housing a hob, sink and classic manual Italian espresso machine, dominates this open-plan loft space. It is supported by a hard-working single bracket on the scuffed steel pillar, which lets light from the wrap-around Crittal windows flow in and add to the airy feel.

opposite A well-appointed wooden shed has been turned into an understatedly glamorous dining space. The white painted wooden boards give a feeling of extra space and light. Their sleek surface is in contrast to the flaky French bistro table stand and the well-scrubbed wooden shelves, which sit solidly under the window. The table has been covered with a plain antique French linen table cloth, while sewing machinists' stools have been made more comfortable with pastel soft Welsh woollen blankets. A rusty brioche tin acts as a suitably themed light shade.

top left A collection of well-used wooden utensils sits in an old brown ceramic jug.

top right Earthy brown salt-glazed pottery contrasts with a shelf of frilly-edged porcelain.

centre left Antique cutlery is ingeniously displayed on a flattened dressing table mirror.

centre right Very plain wooden shelves allow the decorative fluted-edged plates and serving dishes to take the spotlight.

below right Traditional glazed jugs hailing from Apt in the south of France create a still life with some green tomatoes.

deliberately wobbly plates and bowls). What you need to do is decide what things you want to hide away behind cupboard doors and what is going to be out on display. In this case, it's not just down to a matter of taste but one of practicality too – certain items need to be close at hand – knives, for example, are stored perfectly on a professional kitchen-style strong magnetic strip. Track down beautiful old earthenware jugs, creamware pots or old chemists jars in which to store your essential utensils and tomato sauce-stained wooden spoons. They definitely need to be on show, as they're a badge of honour; a sign that you actually do cook in your kitchen! Easily installed slatted metal shelves lend an industrial edge to your kitchen and are great because not only can you stack pots, pans or plates on them but, with the addition of some butcher's-style 'S' hooks, you can suspend things too. Indeed, any hooks that you can fit in your kitchen are sure to be used at some stage. They make the most of the space and work well both in and out of cupboards.

this page A delicious cream Aga is the perfect fit for this old fireplace. A display of silver cups, a candlestick and graphic aluminium letters, along with a string of silvery white shells, lend a relaxed atmosphere to this Cornish kitchen. This feeling is added to by a loosely denim-clad armchair warming itself in the cosy corner.

opposite left Brass lever taps make light work of floury hands.

Choosing a simpler style in your kitchen area means that you don't have to rely on conventional materials or ways of installing them. If you find some beautiful old tiles that you really love but they're a bit too chipped or not in plentiful supply, they will work just as well leaning casually behind your sink space. Or you could decide to ditch tiles altogether; pieces of slate or small, wooden-framed blackboards work well too and are easily cleaned into the bargain. All they need is a quick dunk in a sink full of soapy suds. Extra, flexible storage is always handy. Scratchy metal 'work-in-progress' trolleys on wheels are great for storing everything from plates and stacks of sturdy Duralex café glasses to the contents of your organic vegetable box. They have the obvious benefit of being mobile too. Worn wooden crates are also very useful,

above right Peek into this kitchen and be rewarded by the sight of a pale blue aga. The collection of kettles hints that a cup of tea may be on offer.

as they can be shoved under tables or dressers or stacked neatly in a corner. They could even be mounted on the walls to make an attractive storage area for your vast collection of cookery books, which is handy, as many of us have more of these than we've made hot dinners!

There's nothing better than eating in the garden. A long wooden trestle table is perfect; when the sun comes out you can easily grab the tabletop and its legs from your shed and crowd as many chairs around it as you need. On other, cooler occasions, you might wish to dine in a bit more style than perched on the edge of your kitchen table. Simple textiles such as a slightly crumpled vintage linen makes a great plain tablecloth, allowing your crockery collection and bone-handled cutlery to take pride of place. Wooden curtain rings make unusual napkin holders too, and while on the subject of napkins, old linen tea towels give a little extra coverage for stray crumbs and spills. Folded old Welsh woollen blankets soften the edges of industrial stools or wirework garden chairs. As a finishing touch, add a few candles in confit jars, or decorate the table with a couple of wiry stems in a milk bottle or generous bunches of flowers in a large French ceramic jug or two. It's the perfect setting for an informal, stylishly simple dinner party – all you need now is the food.

THERE'S NOTHING BETTER THAN EATING OUTSIDE. A LONG TRESTLE TABLE IS PERFECT – YOU CAN GRAB IT EASILY FROM THE SHED AND CROWD A STACK OF CHAIRS AROUND IT.

above Make the most of sunny days and take meals outside.

left A long row of curvaceous pastel-painted wooden chairs waits patiently for guests.

right A group of folding chairs gather around a large leafy tree, ready to be collected for lunch.

opposite Weathered Tolix chairs, once painted white but now with a time-worn dappled effect, provide informal seating around a trestle table.

this page A cantilevered lamp by Paolo Rizzatto illuminates this corner, making it an ideal space for reading. The 1930s sofa has been re-covered in beautiful soft brown silk velvet.

opposite above An old gilt-framed mirror, with a scuffed silvered surface, sits on a carved marble fireplace. A woven rug and chunky log baskets give the room a more relaxed feel.

opposite below A grouping of objects on a brushed aluminium table creates an unusual still life, lit by a shiny desk lamp.

Living spaces should be a serene and tranquil domestic landscape where you can escape from the more stressful and busy events of the day, as you sink into the deep, feather-filled cushions piled high on your sofa. They are a place to indulge in your favourite pastimes and guilty pleasures, from listening to music (at full volume if the neighbours don't mind) to quietly reading novels, curled up on your much-loved velvety-soft armchair. They are also often the favoured room for household members to meet up for a cup of tea and a gossip or, if the music is still playing, to dance around energetically until exhaustion strikes and the sofa beckons once more.

Keeping things simple doesn't mean that your home has to be hard-edged or minimal, especially in the one room in the house where you want to kick back and relax. It's a case of carefully choosing your furniture and colour scheme so that nothing jars or feels over the top, and having plenty of storage. The clean lines and light-filled atmosphere of clutter-free spaces are much more relaxing than overly stuffed, overly fussy ones; there's less to worry about as you're not constantly scanning the room for things that need dusting or frills that need flouncing.

living

Don't overload your senses with the latest gadgets or entertainment consoles. It's not that such things are unnecessary or should be banned from stylishly simple homes; sometimes there's nothing better than virtually skiing in your living room on a Sunday afternoon! It's just a

CREATE A COMFORT ZONE BY MAKING THE FIREPLACE THE HEART OF YOUR LIVING SPACE. POSITION YOUR SOFA AND CHAIRS AROUND ITS WARM GLOW.

matter of storing them out of the way when you're not feeling so sporty. Old wooden fruit crates, wicker fishermen's baskets, tin trunks or deed boxes provide contrastingly timeless storage options.

Create a comfort zone by making the fireplace the heart of your living space rather than the television. Position your sofa and chairs around its warm glow. Other than a generously filled log basket, keep the fireplace the very centre of attention. Resist the temptation to fill the mantelshelf with all manner of clutter. Instead, let the simple home ideas of display come into play. If you do feel the need to break up the hard-edged geometry of the fireplace, carefully choose one or two cherished objects that share a certain theme or colour range. They become all the more special this way and the fireplace remains the main attraction.

A generous floor-to-ceiling window means that this huge, light-filled space is the perfect quiet spot for a bit of easy reading. The decorative features such as the fireplace and the cornicing, as well as the antique chair and mirror, are offset by more rustic elements in the room – woven baskets and an enormous rug, a chunky unvarnished table and a casually leaning print – giving the room a relaxing atmosphere.

this page This is a room of pleasing contrasts. Two leather-clad antique chairs on wheels sit on a scrubbed flagstone floor in front of a vast hole-in-the-wall fireplace. The delicate Venetian glass chandelier and abstract painting emphasize the well-loved, time-worn feel of these things.

opposite A utilitarian-looking wood-burning stove sits in a carved marble fireplace. The mantelshelf provides a perch for a group of similarly coloured jugs and a seascape in muted tones. Wide wooden floor-boards add a touch of colour with their warm honey shades.

If your home doesn't come with architectural gems such as a sculptural stone fire surround, a carved wooden one or a decoratively tiled cast-iron Victorian beauty, don't attempt to make up for it by installing replicas. Be true to your home and don't force it into anything that looks unnatural. In any case, a plain, unframed fireplace is the perfect foil for other, more obviously decorative pieces, such as bright cushions or chunkily hand-knitted blankets.

Once you've found your central focus, the sofa, or two sofas if you've got the funds or the space, is the most important piece of furniture in your living area. This is the all-important place to unwind, and needs to be as comfortable as possible. Definitely sit down on any sofas that take your fancy while furniture shopping; you need them to be enduringly comfortable for those long winter evenings or Sunday afternoon movies. A sturdy wooden frame that can withstand the rigours of family life and deep seats with plenty of room for lounging are the hallmarks of a good sofa. A mix of goose and duck feathers makes the most luxurious cushion

this page An inviting slouchy chair encourages relaxation. The whitewashed floorboards and chunky woven seagrass rug add to this feel, along with the soft tones of the painting. Wire in-trays parked by the door are re-employed to hold more fun reading matter than they did in their office days.

opposite This living space is a perfect study in black and white. A deliberately frayed-edged armchair sits next to a more upright classic Robin Day chair. The shelves hold a well-considered collection of monochrome pieces.

opposite Roof lights infuse this small living space with much-needed light. The concrete beam contrasts with the unusual 1950s chandelier.

above A Barcelona chair and stool sit in this light-filled space. The Crittal windows give the room an industrial edge.

filling. They may require a little extra plumping, but it's not the worst job in the world and is definitely worth it. There is a huge array of options out there for covering your sofa – slubby linens and cotton are the most durable choices and in their undyed state sit quietly in a simply decorated living space. But why not take the opportunity to showcase a collection of

vintage textiles that you may have amassed over the years? If you have enough, turn them into a beautiful patchwork sofa cover (if you're not overly familiar with the ways of a sewing machine, find someone who is). Make the most of stitches and seams; these simple details are honest signs of creation, and shouldn't be hidden away. If your textile collection is rather more limited it is easy to create cushion covers that are unique to you and your sofa. Even vintage tea towels can become eye-catching additions to your comfort zone. Old leather sofas add a timeless decadence to your living space, and the older they are, the better they look, proudly showing off the signs and scars of life. Their warm, honey-coloured hues work well with the other natural materials and colours of the simple home.

Always make sure that there are enough cushions to go round and remember that every now and then the floor is the best place to spread out the various sections of the weekend papers. When space is limited or you prefer the look of more upright chairs, it is amazing how easily a cosy woollen blanket casually thrown over one edge of a more austere chair can soften such refined features. If you want to create a slightly more decadent extra seating area, a chaise longue takes up a little less space than another sofa but is a better option for stretching out than an armchair; it looks more relaxed too. An old chaise longue can make a decorative addition to the simplicity of other pieces of furniture in your living space.

As for other furniture, such as low tables that are an essential resting place for trays of coffee and biscuits, go for something with the character that is inherent in antique or rescued pieces, or furniture crafted from recycled elements. Spindly-legged tables with strong shapes that allow light to flood round them are an ideal addition to a living room.

A simple steel-framed daybed with a generously plump mattress covered with Egyptian cotton is a cosy resting spot in this refreshing white space. Extra informal seating is thoughtfully provided with a soft metallic leather pouf and a pile of wheat-filled cushions.

LIVING SPACES SHOULD BE A SERENE AND
TRANQUIL DOMESTIC LANDSCAPE WHERE
YOU CAN ESCAPE FROM THE MORE
STRESSFUL AND BUSY EVENTS OF THE DAY.

DECORATE YOUR LIVING SPACE GENTLY, USING A SOFT PALETTE OF LIGHT-REFLECTING CREAMY WHITES. IT WILL FEEL DELICIOUSLY RELAXING.

Decorate your living space gently, using a soft palette of light-reflecting creamy whites. Large mirrors add sparkle and extra light, while their shabby gilt frames lend them an air of laid-back grandeur. If you can't find a large mirror, hang smaller ones in groups; 1930s-style bevelled-edged ones are particularly good in this situation, as they come in a variety of shapes and sizes.

Getting the lighting right is essential for a relaxing atmosphere. Bright overhead lights seem too harsh when all you want to do is read on the sofa, so fit a dimmer switch; it gives you greater control and is better for the environment. Extra task lighting adds a softer glow just when and where you need it. Articulated anglepoise lamps lend an industrial edge and work surprisingly well with other, more glamorous lighting. A classic crystal chandelier adds elegance to a frugally furnished living space. Its sparkling good looks are all the more elevated when it is the most decorative feature. Chandeliers don't necessarily have to fit into conventional expectations though; well-made plastic or dark flock-finished numbers add an unexpected twist as well as humour.

opposite Black and white makes a dramatic statement, but it doesn't need to feel too austere. A couple of paintings leaning against the wall help to soften the look, along with the quirky addition of a fire bell, presumably there to call for emergency cups of tea.

this page A small writing desk tucked into a corner is an example of well-used space. The tranquil atmosphere of the room is sure to result in well-written letters.

this page Layers of good-quality white linen bedding make for a restful night's sleep. An articulated anglepoise lamp is ideal for bedtime reading, despite its office associations.

opposite above Enclose your bed in soft folds of fabric for an extra-cosy night's sleep.

opposite below Scaffolding poles make a reassuringly sturdy bed frame. Here, woven African textiles and an old grain sack create a fabric headboard and soften the industrial look. The bed is covered with creamy soft linen, and extra warmth is on standby in the form of a pile of striped ticking quilts.

Without a doubt, the bedroom is the one room in the house where comfort is of the uppermost importance. It is the most private space that we have – a comforting place to retreat to at the end of the day – and it is likely that we spend more time there than we do anywhere else. It goes without saying that the bed is the most important piece of furniture in the room. In keeping with the simple home, the best combination is the pairing of a recycled frame, or simply something plain made from wood, with a springy new mattress – a hard-wearing ticking-covered one means that it's ok if its stripey edges are on display. Invest time in researching and selecting the most comfortable mattress for your bed that your budget will allow so that it stands the test of time. If you want something a little more ornate to aid sweet dreams, decorative cast-iron bedsteads often crop up at antique fairs or reclamation yards, though don't expect perfection; these pieces look better and less girly with signs of age and worn-out paint. Also, don't worry if you can't find a matching pair. Not only does this give you the opportunity to think creatively about what could be used in its place but the mismatched arrangement looks all the more relaxed and individual. Just make sure that everything else in the room is kept as pared-down as possible.

bedrooms

Scaffolding poles can be turned into a minimally sculptural bed frame and their hard-edged austerity provides the perfect balance with indulgent piles of super-soft bedding. Their flexibility and extendability means that they could even be used to create a surprisingly fuss-free four-poster, with the addition of some sheer fabric casually draped around the frugal frame. A simple wooden frame, ideally one with a worn, scrubbed surface, has an air of warmth, and the inherent solidity that comes with wood is deeply comforting and reassuring.

Layer upon layer of differently textured textiles turn your bed into a soothing nest; be it a cosy

LAYER UPON LAYER OF NATURAL LINENS AND HANDWOVEN COTTON TURN YOUR BED INTO A SOOTHING NEST.

haven to snuggle deep into during cold winter months or with the option to kick off a layer or two in warmer seasons. Natural linens and handwoven cotton are perfect, as they're unfussy and in their natural state. Their muted tones are soothing and will make your bedroom look more spacious than a bed wrapped in darker shades. Unless you're a particularly heavy sleeper, anything too crazy could be insomnia inducing. The layering of waffle sheets or knobbly knitted blankets on your quilt adds a little something for your senses, while a soft Welsh blanket brings a little muted colour.

Undulating folds of fabric divide the living and sleeping areas of this Parisian apartment. Along with a soft furry throw, they help to create a restful, nest-like sleeping space. The cleverly designed bed incorporates a shelf for bedside lighting, bits and bobs, and the all-important book at bedtime.

this page A simple steel-framed four-poster with buttery linen curtains and layers of feather-filled quilts creates the ultimate classic comfort zone. Draw the curtains and enjoy a quiet, undisturbed night's sleep.

above left This comfortable-looking bed boasts layers of soft brown-coloured quilt covers and sheets, as well as a variety of pleasingly tactile textures, including an extra-chunky hand-knitted blanket in soft porridgey hues. Unusual Perspex shutters allow soft light to filter gently in.

above right The calming stripes of the ticking mattress and softly crumpled linen give an added feeling of relaxation. The stripes on the mattress cover are picked up in the piped cushion edge.

By keeping the walls plain and painting them in pale chalky colours that match your choice of bedding, you are sure to fall asleep quickly.

Windows do need the addition of curtains, but don't choose anything too heavy. It's all the more relaxing to have a little light gently filtering into the room and it keeps us in touch with the rhythms of the seasons. Sheer blinds or panels of muslin draped easily over a curtain pole are the ideal solution if your home is overlooked. To light your way at night, unobtrusive bedside lights set on low tables are just the ticket, especially if they can be angled to the perfect reading position. Make sure that your bedside

table has room for a book at bedtime and your morning cup of tea – if you happen to be lucky enough to have one delivered to your bed! In an ideal world, this would be all the furniture you would have in your cosy bedroom. In this perfect world, you would also have a separate room dedicated to your clothes. However, not many of us are that fortunate, so to house your garments in the style they undoubtedly deserve, look out for an antique French armoire or old shop fittings that have preferably seen slightly better days and are therefore imbued with relaxed grandeur. Your bedroom should now be a beautifully calm haven for a good night's sleep.

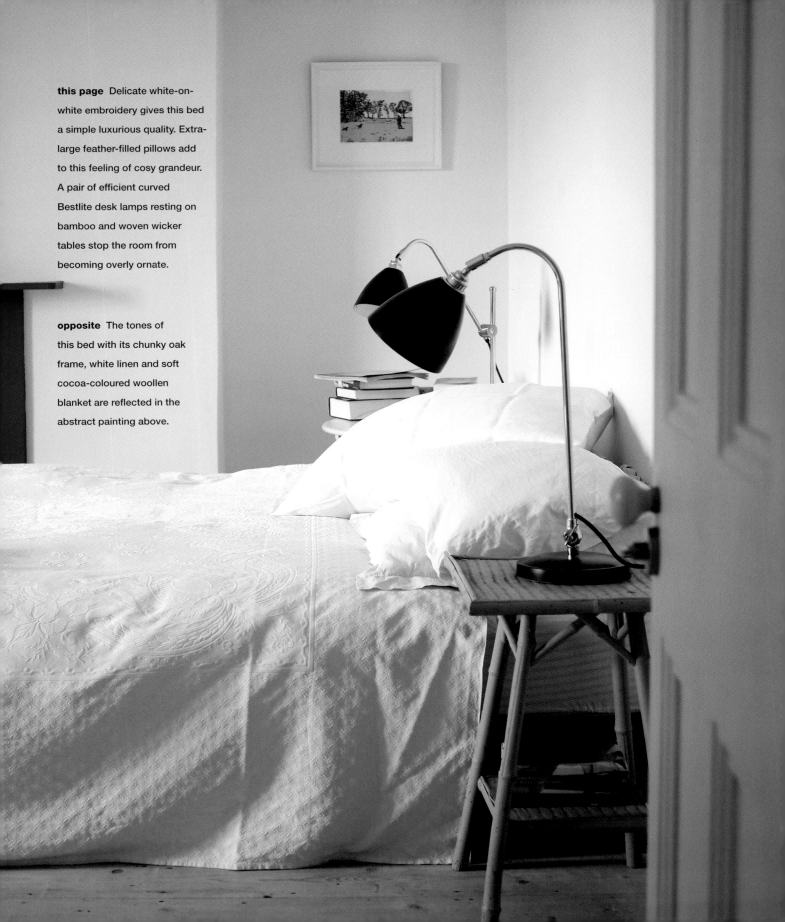

this page Delicate white-on-white embroidery gives this bed a simple luxurious quality. Extra-large feather-filled pillows add to this feeling of cosy grandeur. A pair of efficient curved Bestlite desk lamps resting on bamboo and woven wicker tables stop the room from becoming overly ornate.

opposite The tones of this bed with its chunky oak frame, white linen and soft cocoa-coloured woollen blanket are reflected in the abstract painting above.

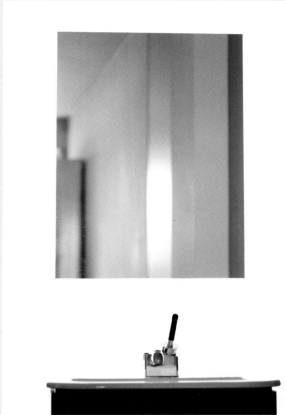

bathrooms

opposite The owners of this Parisian apartment were lucky enough to find this deep, roll-top bathtub at a flea market – it was resurfaced to ensure it lasts another few hundred years. The sink stand was commissioned to reflect the qualities of the tub in a contemporary style.

above left An architectural tap sits below a simple unframed mirror, made by sandwiching it between sheets of glass.

above right Wall-mounted taps add to the illusion of extra space in your bathroom.

The bathroom is the perfect place in which to further your campaign of simplicity. Apply the simple home philosophy for a bathroom with a clean, fresh feel and transform it into a place of sanctuary rather than one of hurried necessity. A well-considered, light, spacious and clutter-free environment is just what you need as you stumble out of bed and begin your bleary-eyed morning ablutions.

Make the most of your space. If you have the room and budget, invest in an ornate roll-top bathtub with clawed feet. It brings old-time glamour into your bathroom and gives you much more room to lie back and relax than narrow, modern acrylic baths.

this page An enormous claw-footed, roll-top bathtub takes pride of place in this bathroom. Its ornate features are contrasted with a sleek Philippe Starck tap, as well as a recycled bath rack made from a sawn piece of ladder cheekily topped with a wire in-tray. A long-handled scrubbing brush sits on a three-legged stool, crusty with layers of splattered paint.

If you want the decadent style of a freestanding bath but want to keep the look a little less ornate, then mount a tub onto sturdy wooden planks. Allow your fabulous bath to take pride of place by paring down other details, otherwise your bathroom might start to feel over the top. The desired look has more in common with rustic simplicity rather than anything too romantic or self-indulgent. Be honest about the functionality of the bathroom; don't box in pipes, as their coppery sheen is another contrasting element in the bathroom and they could be a good place for hanging towels too.

The bathroom is the ideal arena for highly contrasting textures. Wood is a perfect partner for sleek, shiny bathroom fixtures and fittings. Its pleasing weathered warmth brings a nautical feel in a watery context. Introduce pieces of wood creatively, perhaps in the form

top Driftwood makes an unusual splashback with the print block creating a pattern to match. The exposed plaster gives the walls a chalky feel.

centre A curvy cast-iron sink sits on turned legs, allowing light to flow round the room. The tiles against the wall are classic Delft pottery.

of a recycled version of a bath rack made from a sawn section of ladder with a wooden seed tray centre. Also, look out for well-loved wooden stools with flaky paint, splashes and scratches, crates to store your towels or bath-time treats in or an A-frame ladder that makes a simple towel rail leaning casually against the wall. Larger expanses of wood come with your choice of flooring – wooden boards are a good option,

this page Mounted shells and pebbles sit on a simple olive-green cupboard in this nautical, white wood-panelled bathroom. The drop-leaf mahogany table is unusual as these are usually highly polished – this one has a more relaxed feel and fits the room perfectly.

opposite A rescued bath with classic ball and claw feet shows off its essential pipe-work with pride. The theme is continued with the copper pipe towel rack, which sits well next to the rather scientific botanical print.

this page The light in this bathroom is diffused through a sheet of unbleached tissue paper hanging from the window. The old cast-iron and enamel mirror leans casually on the window ledge and provides the perfect counterbalance to the solidly geometric modern sink, as does the large curved shell.

opposite left Old enamel hooks are a useful addition to any bathroom.

either painted white or left in a more natural state. They cope surprisingly well with splashes and spillages; just mop them regularly. It will also help if your bathroom is well ventilated. Poured concrete is another good flooring choice, as its industrial good looks contrast with the more indulgent aspects of bathroom life and it is hard-wearing. Again, just make sure that you look after it properly. Treat with a water-resistant clear sealant; your contractor will help with the details. Also, make sure the finish isn't too smooth or over-polished, as it could be a bit slippery. Whatever you decide, don't be too hard on yourself. A knobbly woolly rug to step onto as you emerge from the bath is warm underfoot and gives your toes a chance to acclimatize.

Sleek modern basins make the most of the space in your bathroom, especially if they are wall-mounted. Their hard-edged modernity

contrasts well with more ornate elements. They can also be adapted to fit in with your particular take on simple style. Mount them on skinny legs to allow light to flood all around, or if you need extra storage, have one fitted onto a cupboard. Basin-style sinks that echo the old porcelain

above Piles of clean, fresh white linen await use. A tiny pair of scissors is an amusing touch, tucked away in the back of this spacious cupboard.

above left Add an air of opulence to your bathroom. Here, a wiry-stemmed bunch of flowers is arranged in a hammered Syrian silver cup resting on a chunky, bleached wooden block.

below left This freestanding bathtub is unusually mounted on pillar-like legs. The extra-wide wooden floorboards and simple towel rail give the room a more relaxed feel in contrast to the imposingly large tub.

A WELL-CONSIDERED, LIGHT, CLUTTER-FREE ENVIRONMENT IS JUST WHAT YOU NEED WHEN YOU STUMBLE OUT OF BED FOR YOUR MORNING ABLUTIONS.

bowl-and-jug washing custom of Victorian times are also an option; you could even go as far as placing two next to each other, his and hers style! Designer chrome taps work well in the simple bathroom too, as their style tends to be pared-down and minimal looking. If you can mount them onto the wall, then do; they look even better when hovering above your basin or tub.

Small details turn your bathroom into your own personal spa. Choose fluffy, undyed organic cotton towels, and find somewhere for a huge, comforting pile of them. Decant bath oils into recycled glass bottles so as to avoid garish plastic packaging spoiling the view from the depths of your tranquil tub. Bathrooms can be another place to display collections of shells and pebbles, or even wooden boats. Put your beachcombing treasures to work; pieces of driftwood lined up behind taps look much more interesting than overly clinical tiles. Don't store your soap in a ready-made soap dish; bowls rescued from the kitchen do the job just as well and often much more stylishly. Beautifully packaged aromatic soaps look like oversized sweets when piled together. Larger metallic bowls give your room an exotic air of the Turkish hamam. Just make sure that you keep the other details plain; one shiny specimen looks all the more special when contrasted in this way.

this page If you have the space, an armchair is a luxurious extra in a bathroom. This one holds a pile of soft towels. Its fuss-free, plain white loose cover adds to the clean lines of this spacious room.

workspaces

this page Patchwork wooden chairs on curved steel former factory frames sit by the window in front of piles of print block. The print block obsession continues on the window blinds, as a couple of pieces have been used as blind pulls.

above left Chunky silver pencils are gathered together in a French confit jar, which sits neatly on a small floating shelf.

above right An array of brushes are organized in small ceramic jars in this studio. Piles of sieves tower above them.

Whether you work at home on a daily basis or just need somewhere to sit and sort out bills, write emails or even actual letters, make sure that this area is in keeping with the rest of your home. The dull grey conventions and uniformity of corporate offices, ugly plastic furniture and flimsy partitions should be avoided at all costs. Choosing more inspirational furniture will aid creativity and won't jar with your personal style. Workspaces can be cleverly tucked into a small corner or even under the stairs or in the garden shed if space is really tight. If this isn't an issue, then devote a whole room to it so that you can close the door on the commotion of family life and get down to business.

The desk is the most important piece of furniture in your workroom, no matter where this happens to be. First of all, choose one that fits into the space. A pair of trestles is particularly flexible; wooden ones are relatively inexpensive and allow light to flow around your table so that it feels less clumpy. But a couple of skinny drawers do the job equally well and provide all-important storage space at the same time. You don't have to stick to conventional tops either. Get the right size piece of wood, patchworked floorboards or maybe a discarded door and you've got a surface on which to work. Old office furniture rescued from obscurity will settle happily into its former habitat; stainless steel 1950s desks are particularly hard-working, or old school-desks

MAKE SURE YOUR WORKSPACE IS IN KEEPING WITH THE REST OF YOUR HOME. CHOOSING MORE INSPIRATIONAL FURNITURE WILL AID CREATIVITY.

may be easier to get your hands on. If not, a simple kitchen table is just as well suited to the task. Old swivel chairs on wheels are much better looking and just as comfortable as modern-day ergonomic alternatives. But it is important to have the right seat at your desk, especially if you're going to be there all day (except for the occasional tea-making trip to the kitchen). Make sure that it's the right height and

your back is properly supported. The addition of linen cushions or maybe a folded blanket will offer extra comfort and soften your workspace.

It's important for both the look of your home and your brain to keep your workspace as clutter free as possible. Keep unruly paperwork at bay by tracking down old filing cabinets. Stripped of their paint they reveal a lovely scratchy, shiny patina, that sits comfortably in

above Sit your desk by a window if possible – natural daylight and an interesting view make working from home a pleasure. In this cleverly appointed writing corner, a large wirework waste basket awaits crumpled mistakes. The spindly legs of the chair and table ensure that the corner doesn't feel over-cluttered.

this page A large desk is constructed from ware boards, rescued from a closed-down pottery factory. A matching pair of steel display cabinets encase treasures, while a shelf close to the roof holds a collection of 1960s vases in various soft shades of blue. These colours are reflected in the sea of the globes sitting on the desk.

enter

This Card is Temporarily Out of Stock

this page This extravagantly articulated draughtsman's table was found in an antique shop in L'Isle sur la Sorgue, Provence.

the simple home. Tin trunks, battered leather suitcases or discarded wooden drawers can also file away your papers with timeless flair. Call on old wire in-trays to store items that you need to be instantly available. They are slim enough to slot under a trestle on the floor or they can rest stylishly on your desk. Pens, pencils and paintbrushes of all shapes and sizes look great gathered together in old jam jars or attractive food tins – much better than in ugly, grey plastic pen holders from the office.

this page The essential paperwork, pencils and pens of the office are tucked away in an old tin trunk, leaving the desk tidy and ready for work. A neat laptop takes less room than an unwieldy computer if space is tight.

BY LIVING WITHOUT EXCESS AND SURROUNDING YOURSELF WITH JUST ENOUGH OF THE RIGHT THINGS, YOU WILL FEEL AN AMAZING SENSE OF SATISFACTION.

above left A quirky desk made from recycled wooden boards on top of a tubular steel sewing machine base creates a neat little workspace. The clever use of space is continued by using the door as a handy blackboard.

above right Why put your pencils in an ugly plastic holder when they could be happily housed in a drilled piece of driftwood?

Decent lighting is vital for your workspace. If you can, place your desk next to a window to make the most of natural daylight; beams of afternoon sun streaming through the window can jolt you out of the worst case of the doldrums. Just don't get too distracted by the goings-on outside. For dark winter days, a desk light is a must. Again, the classic anglepoise is best or you could even go for a trio like on the previous page to make a display of your desk.

Simply styling your workspace and surrounding yourself with well-made, inspirational items will undoubtedly produce the best work. And this goes for the whole of your home. By living without excess and surrounding yourself with just enough of the right things – objects that are personal to you and are thoughtfully designed – you will feel an amazing sense of satisfaction, as well as making your home appear refreshing, relaxing and simple; an easy place to be.

this page This office has found its home tucked away on a landing. Drawers have been slotted under the desk to keep everything as streamlined as possible. A Hans Wegner chair brings a touch of Scandinavian style, with a chunky knitted scarf draped over its shoulders for extra comfort.

sources in the UK

shops and art spaces

Adamczewski
196 High Street
Lewes
East Sussex BN7 2NS
01273 470105
Stylishly simple homewares.

The Art Shop
8 Cross Street
Abergavenny NP7 5EH
www.artshopandgallery.co.uk
01924 832631
Sells artists materials and books.

Baileys
Whitecross Farm
Bridstow
Ross-on-Wye
Herefordshire HR9 6JU
01989 563015
www.baileyshome.com
*Our store – an amazing mix of
everything simple (we are biased).*

Caravan
3 Redchurch Street
Shoreditch
London E2 7DJ
020 7033 3532
www.caravanstyle.com
*Always fascinating. A place
to look at flea-market style.*

The Cloth House
47 & 98 Berwick Street
London W1F 8SJ
020 7437 5155
www.clothhouse.com
*Fabrics from all over the world,
made using and supporting
local craftspeople.*

Contemporary Applied Arts
2 Percy Street
London W1 1DD
020 7436 2344
www.caa.org.uk
*The best of British craft – they also
provide a commissioning service.*

Damson & Slate
10 Market Street
Narbeth
Pembrokeshire SA67 7AU
01437 562058
*Specialising in Welsh art
and craft.*

Frank
65 Harbour Road
Whitstable
Kent CT5 1AG
01227 262500
www.frankworks.eu
*Hand and homemade craft,
decorative pieces and artworks.*

The Gallery
Ruthin Craft Centre
Park Road
Ruthin
Denbighshire LL15 1BB
01824 704774
www.ruthincraftcentre.org.uk
*A state-of-the-art craft centre
with studios, workshops and
three galleries.*

The Hay Makers Gallery
St John's Place
Hay-on-Wye
Herefordshire HR3 5BN
01497 820556
www.haymakers.co.uk
*A co-operative of eight designers
and makers which has been
running for over twenty years.*

Liberty
Regent Street
London W1B 5AH
020 7734 1234
www.liberty.co.uk
*Stylish modern furniture, tableware
and accessories.*

Material
5 Market Street
Ludlow
Shropshire SY8 1BP
01584 876483
www.materialmaterial.com
*Regular shows of painting,
illustration and jewellery.*

Mint
70 Wigmore Street
London W1U 2SF
020 7224 4406
www.mintshop.co.uk
*Modern furniture, ceramics and
accessories.*

St Jude's
Wolterton Road
Itteringham
Norfolk NR11 7AF
01263 587666
www.stjudesgallery.co.uk
*Specialising in British art, craft and
design.*

SCP
135-159 Curtain Road
London EC2A 3BX
020 7739 1869
www.scp.co.uk
*Modern furniture and contemporary
design.*

Selvedge
FREEPOST NAT10681
London N6 5BR
www.selvedge.org
*A magazine about contemporary art
and crafts.*

Shelf
40 Cheshire Street
London E2 6EH
www.helpyourshelf.co.uk
*Handmade books, stationery,
jewellery and ceramic letters.*

Unpackaged
42 Amwell Street
London EC1R 1XT
020 7713 8368
www.beunpackaged.com
*Simple food shopping without all
the unecessary packaging – take
your own containers.*

Yew Tree Gallery
Keigwin
nr Morvah
Pendeen
Cornwall TR19 7TS
01736 786425
www.yewtreegallery.com
*Sculpture, jewellery and
ceramics exhibits.*

Yorkshire Sculpture Park
West Bretton
Wakefield WF4 4LG
01924 832631
www.ysp.co.uk
*A showcase of contemporary
craft and applied arts.*

antique and flea markets

There are many regular antique
fairs around the country. For
information:

www.antiques-atlas.com

www.gbaw.co.uk

markets in London

Portobello
Portobello Road, W11
Saturday, 8am to 5pm.
www.portobelloroad.co.uk

Brick Lane
Brick Lane, Cheshire Street,
Sclater Street, E1 and E2
Sunday, 8am to 2pm.

Bermondsey
Bermondsey Square, SE1
Friday, 4am to 1pm.

Camden
Camden High Street, NW1
Daily.
www.camdenlock.net

Greenwich
Greenwich Church Street,
Stockwell Street,
Greenwich High Road, SE10
*Thursday, Friday, Saturday
& Sunday, 10am to 5pm.*
www.greenwich-market.co.uk

paint

Auro Organic Paints
01452 772020
www.auro.co.uk
*Natural emulsions, eggshells and
chalk paints in muted colours. Also
floor finishes and wood stains.*

Earth Born
01928 734171
www.earthbornpaints.co.uk
Environmentally friendly paints.

sources in the US

furniture and accessories

ABC Carpet & Home

888 Broadway
New York, NY 10003
212 473 3000
Visit the website for a retail outlet
near you.
www.abchome.com
*An eclectic collection of furnishings,
linens, rugs, and other home
accessories.*

Anthropologie

85 Fifth Avenue
New York, NY 10003
212 627 5885
Visit the website to find
a store near you.
www.anthropologie.com
*One-of-a-kind home accessories,
including decorative hooks, boxes,
cupboard knobs, and racks.*

The Conran Shop

Bridgemarket
407 East 59th Street
New York, NY 10022
866 755 9079
www.conranusa.com
*Modern furniture for every room,
plus storage items.*

Fishs Eddy

889 Broadway
New York, NY 10003
212 420 9020
www.fishseddy.com
*Overstock supplies of simple plates
and other tableware.*

Knoll

Phone 800 343 5665 or visit the
website for showrooms.
www.knoll.com
Modern and ergonomic lamps.

Moenia Design

415 240 4540
Visit the website for a retail outlet
near you.
www.moeniadesign.com
*A wide selection of baskets
for storage and style.*

Ochre

462 Broome Street
New York, NY 10013
212 414 4332
www.ochre.net
*Contemporary furniture, antiques,
accessories, and lighting.*

Pottery Barn

1965 Broadway
New York, NY 10023
212 579 8477
www.potterybarn.com
*Contemporary furniture and
accessories for the home.*

R 20th Century Design

82 Franklin Street
New York, NY 10013
212 343 7979
www.r20thcentury.com
*Includes a comprehensive selection
of mid-century lamps and lighting
fixtures.*

Restoration Hardware

935 Broadway
New York, NY 10010
212 260 9479
Visit the website for an outlet near
you.
www.restorationhardware.com
*Fine hardware, including lighting,
furniture, and accessories for the
home.*

Takashimaya

693 Fifth Avenue
New York, NY 10022
212 350 0100
www.takashimaya-ny.com
*Home and garden accessories
and floristry.*

flea markets

The Annex Antique Fair and Flea Market

West 39th Street and Ninth Avenue,
New York
212 243 5343
www.hellskitchenfleamarket.com
*Manhattan's primary flea market
takes place every Saturday and
Sunday.*

Brimfield Antique Show

Route 20
Brimfield, MA 01010
www.brimfieldshow.com
*This famous flea market, which
features dealers from all over the
U.S. and from Europe, runs for a
week in May, July, and September.*

Englishtown Auction Sales

90 Wilson Avenue
Englishtown, NJ 07726
732 446 9644
www.englishtownauction.com
*This 100-acre market attracts
professional and amateur dealers.
Open Saturday and Sunday,
year-round.*

Rose Bowl Flea Market

100 Rose Bowl Drive
Pasadena, CA
323 560 7469
www.rgcshows.com
*On the second Sunday of every
month, everything from retro kitsch
to fine furnishings.*

architectural salvage, restoration, and antiques

Architectural Accents

2711 Piedmont Road NE
Atlanta, GA 30305
404 266 8700
www.architecturalaccents.com
*Antique light fixtures, door
hardware, garden antiques, and
other reclaimed items.*

Architectural Paneling, Inc.

979 Third Avenue
New York, NY 10022
212 371 9632
www.apaneling.com
*Reproduction fireplaces, paneling,
and moldings.*

Caravati's Inc.

104 East Second Street
Richmond, VA 23224
804 232 4175
www.caravatis.com
*Restoration materials and
architectural details from
old buildings.*

Clawfoot Supply

at Signature Hardware
2700 Crescent Springs Pike
Erlanger, KY 41017
866 855 2284
www.clawfootsupply.com
*Authentic reproduction clawfoot
tubs, pedestal and console sinks,
Topaz copper soaking tubs, and
more.*

Harrington Brass Works

201 818 1300
www.harringtonbrassworks.com
*Brass fixtures for kitchen and home,
especially faucets. Also bathroom
products.*

Salvage One Architectural Elements

1840 W. Hubbard
Chicago, IL 60622
312 733 0098
www.salvageone.com
Architectural artifacts.

paint

Benjamin Moore Paints

161 6th Ave
New York, NY 10013
Visit the website for stockists.
www.benjaminmoore.com
Fine paints.

The Old Fashioned Milk Paint Company

436 Main Street
Groton, MA 01450
978 448 6336
www.milkpaint.com
*These paints, made from natural
pigments, replicate the color and
finish of Colonial and Shaker
antiques.*

picture credits

Key: a=above, b=below, r=right, l=left, c=centre.

All photography by Debi Treloar.

Page 1 Khadi & Co., by Bess Nielsen; **2** Hélène & Konrad Adamczewski, Lewes; **3** Mark & Sally Bailey's home in Herefordshire; **4** The London home of stylist/designer Janie Jackson of Parma Lilac; **5** The London home of one of the owners of Ochre; **6** The London home of stylist/designer Janie Jackson of Parma Lilac; **7** Hélène & Konrad Adamczewski, Lewes; **8al** Mark & Sally Bailey's home in Herefordshire; **8br** Hélène & Konrad Adamczewski, Lewes; **9** The London home of stylist/designer Janie Jackson of Parma Lilac; **10** Mark & Sally Bailey's home in Herefordshire; **11** The family home of Julia Bird in Cornwall; **12–13** The home and studio of Julian Stair in London; **14** The family home of Julia Bird in Cornwall; **15l** The home of the designer Edith Mézard in Lumières; **15r** Mark & Sally Bailey's home in Herefordshire; **16l** The family home of Julia Bird in Cornwall; **16r** Hélène & Konrad Adamczewski, Lewes; **17** The family home of Julia Bird in Cornwall; **18** "Chambre de séjour avec vue…", Saignon in Luberon; **19al** The home and studio of Julian Stair in London; **19ar&br** The family home of Julia Bird in Cornwall; **19bl** The home of the designer Edith Mézard in Lumières; **20bl** The home of the designer Edith Mézard in Lumières; **20br** "Chambre de séjour avec vue…", Saignon-en-Luberon; **21l** Hélène & Konrad Adamczewski, Lewes; **21r** Khadi & Co., by Bess Nielsen; **22** "Chambre de séjour avec vue…", Saignon-en-Luberon; **23l** Mark & Sally Bailey's home in Herefordshire; **23c** "Chambre de séjour avec vue…", Saignon-en-Luberon; **23r** Sharon & Paul Mrozinski's home in Bonnieux, France; **24l** Le Café Chinois, 7 rue de Bearn, 75003 Paris, owned by Catherine and Pierre Langlois; **24r** "Chambre de séjour avec vue…", Saignon-en-Luberon; **25** The London home of stylist/designer Janie Jackson of Parma Lilac; **26al** Sharon & Paul Mrozinski's home in Bonnieux, France; **26ac** Hélène & Konrad Adamczewski, Lewes; **26ar** "Chambre de séjour avec vue…", Saignon-en-Luberon; **26bl** Le Café Chinois, 7 rue de Bearn, 75003 Paris, owned by Catherine and Pierre Langlois; **26br** The home and studio of Julian Stair in London; **27** Sharon & Paul Mrozinski's home in Bonnieux, France; **28–29** The London home of one of the owners of Ochre; **30 & 31r** The London home of stylist/designer Janie Jackson of Parma Lilac; **31l** Le Café Chinois, 7 rue de Bearn, 75003 Paris, owned by Catherine and Pierre Langlois; **32–33** Hélène & Konrad Adamczewski, Lewes; **33r** The London home of stylist/designer Janie Jackson of Parma Lilac ; **34** The home and studio of Julian Stair in London; **35** The home of the designer Edith Mézard in Lumières; **36** The London home of stylist/designer Janie Jackson of Parma Lilac; **37l** Hélène & Konrad Adamczewski, Lewes; **37r** Khadi & Co., by Bess Nielsen; **38** Hélène & Konrad Adamczewski, Lewes; **39al** Mark & Sally Bailey's home in Herefordshire; **39ar** Khadi & Co., by Bess Nielsen; **39b** The family home of Julia Bird in Cornwall; **40a & 41** The home and studio of Julian Stair in London; **40b** The London home of stylist/designer Janie Jackson of Parma Lilac; **42al** Khadi & Co., by Bess Nielsen; **42ar** Mark & Sally Bailey's home in Herefordshire; **42c** Hélène & Konrad Adamczewski, Lewes; **42bl** Mark & Sally Bailey's home in Herefordshire; **42br** The home of the designer Edith Mézard in Lumières; **43al** Mark & Sally Bailey's home in Herefordshire; **43ar** Hélène & Konrad Adamczewski, Lewes; **43b** Khadi & Co., by Bess Nielsen; **44–45a** Mark & Sally Bailey's home in Herefordshire; **45b** The London home of Richard Moore; **46r** Mark & Sally Bailey's home in Herefordshire; **47** Sharon & Paul Mrozinski's home in Bonnieux; **48a&cl** The London home of Richard Moore; **48cr** Mark & Sally Bailey's home in Herefordshire; **48b** "Chambre de séjour avec vue…", Saignon-en-Luberon; **49** Mark & Sally Bailey's home in Herefordshire; **50** The family home of Julia Bird in Cornwall; **51l** The home of the designer Edith Mézard in Lumières; **51r** Caravane by François Dorget; **52** Caravane by François Dorget; **53** Sharon & Paul Mrozinski's home in Bonnieux; **54al** Caravane by François Dorget; **54ac** The London home of stylist/designer Janie Jackson of Parma Lilac; **54ar&b** Khadi & Co., by Bess Nielsen; **55** The Paris home of architects Anki Linde & Pierre Saalburg of lsl architects; **56** Mark & Sally Bailey's home in Herefordshire; **57l** The home of the designer Edith Mézard in Lumières; **57r** Hélène & Konrad Adamczewski, Lewes; **58a & 59** Mark & Sally Bailey's home in Herefordshire; **58b** The family home of Julia Bird in Cornwall; **60** Mark & Sally Bailey's home in Herefordshire; **61l** Khadi & Co., by Bess Nielsen; **61r** The home of the designer Edith Mézard in Lumières; **62** The London home of stylist/designer Janie Jackson of Parma Lilac; **63l** Le Café Chinois, 7 rue de Bearn, 75003 Paris, owned by Catherine & Pierre Langlois; **63r** "Chambre de séjour avec vue…", Saignon-en-Luberon; **64** The family home of Julia Bird in Cornwall; **66–67** Mark & Sally Bailey's home in Herefordshire; **67br** The London home of Richard Moore; **68** The London home of stylist/designer Janie Jackson of Parma Lilac; **69** Mark & Sally Bailey's home in Herefordshire; **70** Sharon & Paul Mrozinski's home in Bonnieux, France; **71** The London home of one of the owners of Ochre; **72** Sharon & Paul Mrozinski's home in Bonnieux, France; **73** Hélène & Konrad Adamczewski, Lewes; **74 & 75l** The London home of stylist/designer Janie Jackson of Parma Lilac; **75r** The London home of Richard Moore; **76** The family home of Julia Bird in Cornwall; **77** The London home of stylist/designer Janie Jackson of Parma Lilac; **78l** The home and studio of Julian Stair in London; **78–79** The London home of Richard Moore; **79ar** The family home of Julia Bird in Cornwall; **79br & 80** The London home of Richard Moore; **81al** Mark & Sally Bailey's home in Herefordshire; **81ac** The family home of Julia Bird in Cornwall; **81ar** Sharon & Paul Mrozinski's home in Bonnieux, France; **81bl** The London home of Richard Moore; **81br** Mark & Sally Bailey's home in Herefordshire; **82–83** The family home of Julia Bird in Cornwall; **84–85** The London home of stylist/designer Janie Jackson of Parma Lilac; **86al** The Paris home of architects Anki Linde & Pierre Saalburg of lsl architects; **86ar** Khadi & Co., by Bess Nielsen; **86b** The London home of one of the owners of Ochre; **87l&r** Mark & Sally Bailey's home in Herefordshire; **87c** The London home of one of the owners of Ochre; **88–89** Hélène & Konrad Adamczewski, Lewes; **90** "Chambre de séjour avec vue…", Saignon-en-Luberon; **91bl** The London home of Richard Moore; **91br** Sharon & Paul Mrozinski's home in Bonnieux, France; **92a** The home and studio of Julian Stair in London; **92b** The home of the designer Edith Mézard in Lumières; **93** The family home of Julia Bird in Cornwall; **94** Sharon & Paul Mrozinski's home in Bonnieux, France; **95a** The London home of Richard Moore; **95bl** The Paris home of architects Anki Linde & Pierre Saalburg of lsl architects; **95br** Hélène & Konrad Adamczewski, Lewes; **96** Mark & Sally Bailey's home in Herefordshire; **97** The home of the designer Edith Mézard in Lumières; **98–99** The Paris home of architects Anki Linde & Pierre Saalburg of lsl architects; **100** Hélène & Konrad Adamczewski, Lewes; **101–102l** Le Café Chinois, 7 rue de Bearn, 75003 Paris, owned by Catherine and Pierre Langlois; **102r–103** The home and studio of Julian Stair in London; **104–105** The London home of one of the owners of Ochre, www.ochre.net; **106** Mark & Sally Bailey's home in Herefordshire; **107al, cr&b** Sharon & Paul Mrozinski's home in Bonnieux, France; **107cl** The London home of stylist/designer Janie Jackson of Parma Lilac; **108al** Mark & Sally Bailey's home in Herefordshire; **108ar&c** Le Café Chinois, 7 rue de Bearn, 75003 Paris, owned by Catherine and Pierre Langlois; **108bl** The London home of Richard Moore; **108br** The home and studio of Julian Stair in London; **109** Mark & Sally Bailey's home in Herefordshire; **110** The family home of Julia Bird in Cornwall; **112–113** "Chambre de séjour avec vue…", Saignon-en-Luberon; **114–115b** The Paris home of architects Anki Linde & Pierre Saalburg of lsl architects; **115r–117** Hélène & Konrad Adamczewski, Lewes; **119–120** Hélène & Konrad Adamczewski, Lewes; **121** The London home of Richard Moore; **122–123** The London home of one of the owners of Ochre; **124–125** The London home of stylist/designer Janie Jackson of Parma Lilac; **126–127** Hélène & Konrad Adamczewski, Lewes; **128** The family home of Julia Bird in Cornwall; **129al** Sharon & Paul Mrozinski's home in Bonnieux, France; **129br** Mark & Sally Bailey's home in Herefordshire; **130–131** The Paris home of architects Anki Linde & Pierre Saalburg of lsl architects; **132&133r** Sharon & Paul Mrozinski's home in Bonnieux, France; **133l** The London home of stylist/designer Janie Jackson of Parma Lilac; **134l** The London home of one of the owners of Ochre; **134–135** Hélène & Konrad Adamczewski, Lewes; **136–137** The Paris home of architects Anki Linde & Pierre Saalburg of lsl architects; **138–139 a&bl** Mark & Sally Bailey's home in Herefordshire; **140–141** The family home of Julia Bird in Cornwall; **142&143l** Hélène & Konrad Adamczewski, Lewes; **143r** The home of the designer Edith Mézard in Lumières; **144a&145** The London home of stylist/designer Janie Jackson of Parma Lilac; **146–147l** Mark & Sally Bailey's home in Herefordshire; **147r** The home and studio of Julian Stair in London; **148** Hélène & Konrad Adamczewski, Lewes; **149** Mark & Sally Bailey's home in Herefordshire; **150** Sharon & Paul Mrozinski's home in Bonnieux, France; **151–152** Mark & Sally Bailey's home in Herefordshire; **153** The London home of stylist/designer Janie Jackson of Parma Lilac. **Endpapers:** The family home of Julia Bird, Cornwall.

businesses whose work is featured in this book

Adamczewski
196 High Street
Lewes
East Sussex BN7 2NS
*Pages 2, 7, 8br, 16r, 21l,
26ac, 32–33, 37l, 38, 42c, 43ar,
57r, 73, 88–89, 95b, 100,
115r–117, 119–120, 126–127,
134–135, 142 & 143l, 148*

Baileys
Whitecross Farm
Bridstow
Ross-on-Wye
Herefordshire HR9 6JU
+44 (0)1989 563015
www.baileyshome.com
*Pages 3, 8al, 10, 15r, 23l, 39ar,
42ar, 42bl, 43al,
44–45a, 46r, 48cr, 49, 56, 58a,
59, 60, 66–67, 69, 81al, 81br,
87l&r, 96, 106, 108al, 109,
129br, 138–139a, 139bl, 146,
147l, 149, 151–152*

bird...inspired by nature
3 Custom House Hill
Fowey
Cornwall PL23 1AB
+44 (0) 1726 833737
&
49 Molesworth Street
Wadebridge
Cornwall PL27 7DR
info@birdkids.co.uk
www.birdkids.co.uk
*Pages 11, 14, 16l, 17, 19ar &
br, 39b, 50, 58b, 64, 76, 79ar,
81ac, 82–83, 93, 110, 128,
140–141*

Le Café Chinois
Café Salon de Thés
Boutique Objets d'Asie
7, rue de Béarn
75003 Paris
+33 (0) 1 42 71 47 43
www.lecafechinois.fr
*Pages 24l, 26bl, 31l, 63l, 101,
102l, 108ar, 108c*

Caravane
6 rue Pavée
75004 Paris
+33 (0) 1 44 61 04 20
Pages 51r, 52, 54al

**"Chambre de séjour avec
vue…" – Demeure d'art et
d'hôtes**
84400 Saignon-en-Lubéron
France
www.chambreavecvue.com
*Pages 18, 20br, 22, 23c, 24r,
26ar, 48b, 63r, 90, 112–113*

**Khadi & Co
By Bess Nielsen**
Emporium
37 rue Debelleyme
75003 Paris
France
Open Wed–Sat,
11am–7pm
+33 (0) 1 42 74 71 32
fax +33 (0) 1 44 59 84 65
khadiandco@hotmail.com
www.khadiandco.com
*Pages 1, 21r, 37r, 39ar, 42al,
43b, 54ar&b, 61l, 86ar*

Isl architects
33 rue d'Hauteville
75010 Paris
+33 (0) 1 48 00 09 65
fax +33 (0) 1 48 00 09 31
www.lslarchitects.com
*Pages 55, 86al, 95bl, 98–99,
114–115b, 130–131, 136–137*

Edith Mézard
Chateau de L'Ange
84220 Lumières
France
Shop open daily,
3pm-7.30pm
*Pages 15l, 19bl, 20bl, 35, 42br,
51l, 57l, 61r, 92b, 97, 143r.*

Richard Moore
Creative Consultant to the
Retail Industry
Scenographic
+44 (0)7958 740045
www.scenographic.blogspot.com
*Pages 45b, 48a, 48cl, 67br,
75r, 78–79, 79br, 80, 81bl,
91bl, 95a, 108bl, 121*

Sharon & Paul Mrozinski
The Marston House
Main Street at Middle Street
PO Box 517
Wiscasset
Maine 04578
+ 1 207 882 6010
fax + 1 207 882 6965
sharon@marstonhouse.com
www.marstonhouse.com
*Pages 23r, 26al, 27, 47, 53, 70,
72, 81ar, 91r, 94, 107al, 107cr,
107b, 129al, 132, 133r, 150*

Ochre London Ltd.
+44 (0)870 787 9242
www.ochre.net
*Pages 5, 28–29, 71, 86b, 87c,
104–105, 122–123, 134l*

Parma Lilac
98 Chepstow Road
London W10 6EP.
(Visits by appointment)
+44 (0)20 7912 0882
info@parmalilac.co.uk
www.parmalilac.co.uk
*Pages 4, 6, 9, 25, 30, 31r, 33r,
36, 40b, 54ac, 62, 68, 74–75l,
77, 84–85, 107cl, 124–125,
133l, 144a, 145, 153*

Julian Stair
Studio
52a Hindmans Road
London SE22 9NG
+44 (0)20 8693 4877
studio@julianstair.com
www.julianstair.com
*Pages 12–13, 19al, 26br, 34,
40a, 41, 78l, 92a, 102r, 103,
108br, 147r*

index

acknowledgments

This book was a hectic scramble around London, Paris, Cornwall, Herefordshire and the south of France. There was much refilling of London parking meters and losing our way in narrow cobbled streets in Paris, while staggering under the weight of all the bags and photographic equipment! But it was definitely worth it as we were allowed into some perfect simple spaces – so a big thank you to all those people who let us take over their homes for a day…especially:

Hélène & Konrad Adamczewski, a lesson in restraint. Thank you for lunch.

Richard Moore, creative consultant, an amazing lesson in how to use a small space.

Janie Jackson, Parma Lilac showroom open by appointment.

Solenne da la Fouchardière, designer & part of the Ochre co-operative, London & New York.

Julian Stair & Claire Wilcox, we'd like to be buried in one of Julian's stunning sarcophagi.

Gum & Julia Bird, good luck with the new shop. A huge thanks for supper and lunch.

Ken & Susan Briggs, so kind and generous, huge patrons of the arts.

Pierre Jaccaud, Chambre de séjour avec vue. Bed, art and breakfast – a lesson in curating.

Bess Nielsen of Khadi & Co., the veritable queen of hand-spun, hand-dyed textiles.

Anki Linde & Pierre Saalburg of lsl architectures, we are in awe of their attention to detail.

Edith Mézard, who let us into her home, showroom and studio with the added bonus of her son's neighbouring restaurant, Le Garage.

Caravane, inspirational furniture and textile showroom.

Sharon and Paul Mronzinski, just brilliant.

Mark and Sally would also like to thank Alison, Leslie, Delphine, Paul and Jess (thanks for putting up with us again) and everyone else at Ryland Peters & Small.

Debi Treloar – a brilliant photographer and calm in all situations, which makes her a joy to work with. Also her assistant Lorna, who made us laugh, while remaining amazingly focused.

Huge thanks to Charlotte Farmer who wrote the words over copious coffees in our café.

Last but not least, thanks to Ben, Lucy, Laura, Kirstin and everyone at Baileys.